Albert R. Taylor

The study of the child;

A brief treatise on the psychology of the child, with suggestions for teachers,

students, and parents;

Albert R. Taylor

The study of the child;
A brief treatise on the psychology of the child, with suggestions for teachers, students, and parents;

ISBN/EAN: 9783337818760

Printed in Europe, USA, Canada, Australia, Japan

Cover: Foto ©ninafisch / pixelio.de

More available books at **www.hansebooks.com**

THE STUDY
OF THE CHILD

A BRIEF TREATISE ON THE
PSYCHOLOGY OF THE CHILD

WITH SUGGESTIONS FOR
TEACHERS, STUDENTS, AND PARENTS

BY

A. R. TAYLOR, Ph. D.

PRESIDENT OF THE STATE NORMAL SCHOOL
EMPORIA, KANSAS

NEW YORK
D. APPLETON AND COMPANY
1899

EDITOR'S PREFACE.

In my preface to this sound and wholesome book on child study I will present some thoughts on the symbolic and conventional stages of mind in childhood and on the process by which the child outgrows the symbolic stage of mind. I will then consider the doctrine that concepts are mental images and bring forward the theory that they are not mental images but definitions, and conclude by discussing imitation as the chief activity of the child in play and point out the change by which it becomes originality.

The earlier period of infancy, say up to the age of six, with average children has been called the symbolic stage, while the later stage, which begins somewhere about six and lasts through life, is called the " conventional " stage.

We commonly use the word *symbolic* in a restricted sense—namely, to signify the use of some material object to present an invisible spiritual object. The wind blows and shows power. It can not be seen, and yet it moves things that can be seen. The breath too is a sort of wind, invisible and yet powerful. The soul moves the body and yet is not seen; it is a sort of wind; it is the

v

breath. Such was the infantile way of thinking.
Anima, the breath, was used to symbolize the soul.
Its root is a word signifying the blowing of the
wind.

The constant use of the symbol tends to con-
vert it into a conventional sign of the spiritual
meaning. *Anima* at first conveyed the idea of
breath, before passing to that of soul. The mind
gradually shortened its contemplation of the physical meaning and prolonged its stay on the spiritual meaning and laid greater stress on it. By
and by it forgot altogether the physical or material meaning, and went from the word directly to
the idea of vital energy moving the body and pos-
sessing thought and feeling. So at last the word
anima came to be the conventional sign for soul
and lost its symbolic use. The material meaning
was forgotten.

With increasing strength of mind the child
grasps relations more and more fully, and by this
his conceptions become less and less mere pictures.
This is the way that he outgrows the symbolic
stage of thought.

To illustrate this process of growth, consider
the chain of causality involved in thinking the familiar object *bread*. This illustration is used by
Professor Noiré to explain apperception. Going
backward toward the origin of bread we have successive steps of baking, kneading the dough, mix-
ing the meal or flour with yeast, lard, butter, and
other ingredients, the grinding of the grain and
sifting the meal, the harvesting of the grain with
all its details of cutting, binding sheaves, thresh-

ing, etc., the earlier processes of plowing, harrow-
ing, sowing the grain, its growth dependent on
rain and sunshine. Each one of these links in
the chain has side relations to other chains of
causality; for example, the yeast put into the
bread connects it with hops or some other ferment
or effervescent, the lard connects bread with the series of ideas involved in pork-raising, the salt with
salt manufacture, the baking with the structure
of the oven and the fuel. The retrograde series
toward the origin is matched with a progressive
series toward the future use of the bread. There is
the preparation for the table, the set meals, the
eating and digestion, the sustenance of life, the
strength acquired, the work accomplished by
means of it, etc.

This chain of causation is symbolized in the
story of the House that Jack Built and similar
inventions.

In play the child lets one thing stand for another, and "makes believe," for instance, that
this mud is dough; it can be dried or baked too.
But here the chain of causality departs from that
of bread. The child can not eat the mud loaf.
The mud was not made of meal, flour, yeast, lard,
and salt like dough.

The child begins play by making believe that
something is something else, when there is very
little resemblance. It is nearly all make-believe
at first. But he makes progress by demanding
an increase of resemblance. He takes any stick
for a horse at first: then he prefers a stick with
a horse's head. Then no stick will do, but he

must have a hobbyhorse on rockers, with saddle and bridle, and he imitates a gallop by rocking to and fro. His enjoyment of his play was greatest when he had the most make-believe in it. In proportion as he introduces real steps of causality he loses the educative effect of play and he gets less amusement from it. For his enjoyment and educational advantage is proportioned to the amount his imagination is exercised. When he receives a finished hobbyhorse, with real saddle and bridle and other completed reproductions of the real horse, there is less for his imagination. He soon wearies of the finished, elaborate plaything.

The child at first understands a very small fragment of the entire process of production of a thing. He pretends that a crooked stick is a scythe. But he is helped by this plaything to understand what is necessary for the real object, the scythe. It must have a blade, and he has a wooden one fastened to his crooked stick. Then he becomes impressed with the necessity of having a blade that will cut. If he gets this he gets a real scythe, and his play has converted itself into work.

It is the dialectic process of play that it end by becoming work. Carry out the practice of anything and its natural results are its dialectic. The child starts with a stick for a horse and ends only with getting a real horse to ride and drive. There were many steps on the way: First a horse's head to his stick, then a bridle and a whip, then a chair represents a horse and wagon, then a playmate is harnessed as a horse, then a hobbyhorse with all the limbs of a horse and with a close imitation of external appearance, then perhaps a dog or a goat harnessed to a toy wagon, then the real horse.

All the steps in the ascent involve new concepts of what is necessary to the real causality. In a causation series the child can now think by definitions and not merely by pictures. This matter of thinking-by-definitions ought to be carefully studied by the teacher in the primary school.

The belief that concepts or general notions are mental images is very prevalent among psychologists. But it would be more correct to say that general notions are not mental images so much as definitions. A definition must state an identity with something else, and a difference. In a mere mental picture identity and difference are not distinctly brought to attention. In the symbolic stage of the mind the distinction between the particular individual and the general class is not fully developed. When the child plays or makes believe that this stick is a horse, the identity is brought out, but the difference is kept out of sight and ignored. When the soul is compared to breath and the breath is made a symbol of the soul, a slender thread of identity is brought into prominence and the vast field of difference is dropped out of sight. The progress of the child in power of thought is indicated by his ability to analyze by separating the sameness, identity, or resemblance from the differences which manifest themselves. When the child notes a resemblance and classifies an object, and at the

same time notes differences, he has arrived at the
stage in which he thinks a definition. The definition first states the object's identity or resemblance to something else, and secondly points out
the difference. This is a bird, it is yellow. The
result is the concept yellow bird; general class,
bird; difference or limitation of the class bird to
birds of a yellow color. This bird is an eagle,
this bird is bald-headed: result, definition of the
subclass, bald-headed eagle.

Now, it is important in entering upon child
study to note carefully the difference between
thinking with an image and thinking-with-a-defi-
nition. The mind of the person mature in
thought as well as the mind of the first beginner
forms images when he thinks general notions or
concepts, but the mature thinker will notice that
when he thinks an image he immediately notes its
limitations and its inadequateness to correspond to
the general definition which constitutes the essential part of the general notion. When the word
" horse " is mentioned I think at first of a gray
horse, then I notice that I am imaging a special
kind of horse and I imagine a sorrel-colored horse,
and then a larger horse; one in the attitude of
standing still, another in the attitude of running
fast. A series of images are formed and dismissed
as quickly as formed. In this the mind acts without reflecting upon its action. It makes images
and at the same time notes that these images are
mere examples or illustrations of the general concept, and that they do not exhaust it.

The child at first forms vague and general notions. He does not seize particular objects with all their distinguishing characteristics. He makes out only a very few general marks or attributes. He classes together objects which a more experienced power of thought distinguishes.

Just as the child loses his interest in play when he comes to recognize numerous steps in the causation process, so the child gives up his symbolic thinking, and with it his exclusive reliance on mental pictures, when he comes to notice not only identities but differences. His first definitions are those founded on external appearance. But with the growth of his mind and the observation of the process of causation he comes to note the function of the object and its actions, and he makes his definitions describe acts of causation. With his progress in observing causation the child attains independence of thinking and confidence in himself.

Imitation partakes of the nature of symbolizing, and it forms a very large element in play. It marks the first beginnings of education. The child who begins to imitate gives evidence of self-consciousness. He notices the activity of another fellow-being and recognizes that activity as proceeding from an energy or will power akin to the power which he himself possesses. He proves to himself the possession of that power by imitating the action in which he is interested. It is evident that imitation, therefore, is a kind of spiritual assimilation, a digesting and making one's own of the act of another. Of course, the purpose is not conscious, but it is really present all the same.

Whenever children show a passionate interest in discovering properties and qualities in things it is high time for them to leave the kindergarten and take up the work of learning conventional signs, reading, writing, arithmetic, the technical terms of geography, etc.

So, too, whenever the child loves to trace chains of causation by noticing the effect of other objects upon the thing which he is studying, and when he loves to trace out the effects of the function of his object upon its environment, we note the same ripeness and maturity of the child which enables him to take up work beyond the scope of the kindergarten. Such a child can not find symbolic plays and games perfectly congenial to him. He has obtained a higher stage of individual culture and seeks gratification which comes from testing his power of analysis on the external world. He has come to a stage of thinking above the symbolic.

The child outgrows his feeble state of mind, wherein he takes the dead result for the true reality, and gradually acquires the ability to think the forces and powers, the causal energies, which bring things into existence and transform those things into other things.

Imitation has the same course of development as the symbolic thought which passes over into thinking-by-definitions. At first imitation copies the merest external appearances. But it gradually gets possession of the motives and purposes of the action; finally, the imitator may arrive at the fundamental principle which originates the action.

Then the imitator finds no longer his guide and rule in an external model. He finds the rule for his action in his own mind and becomes original.

The child imitates an external object. It may be another person or it may be an animal or a thing. His imitation is, as I have said, an act of assimilation, an act of making for himself that which he sees made by another, and thereby proving his own causative power. By this action of imitation he therefore grows toward the feeling of responsibility. The act as performed by another is none of his. The act as imitated by himself is his own and he is responsible for it. Imitation is therefore an act of the will, just as symbolism and thinking-by-definitions is an act of the intellect. But the first beginnings of imitation deal with the merest externalities of the action imitated. It is the "dialectic" of imitation to leave these externals and strive for a more and more internal relation toward that which it imitates. It seizes the motives and purposes of the action and it sees the logical necessity for these purposes and motives. It connects them more and more with its own fundamental principle of action. At last, when it performs the imitated act as an expression of its own purposes and convictions, imitation has become originality.

The child should not be hastened unduly in his progress out of symbolism. As long as he has interest and a real delight in the symbol he should be indulged in its employment. So, too, with regard to imitation. The judicious teacher will not seek to deepen the child's insight into motives

2

and purposes and arouse a too early feeling of responsibility in his mind.   In most cases the pressure of the society in which the child lives—a society mostly of grown persons possessed of a deep
feeling of responsibility—will hasten the child's
development into a view of moral purpose quite
soon enough.

·   W. T. Harris. -

Washington, D. C., *May 12, 1898.*

EXPLANATORY.

For twenty years the subject of Child Study has been growing into prominence in all parts of this country, and many interesting and valuable papers and reports on various phases of the subject have been published from time to time in leading educational journals. Child study societies have been formed in scores of cities, and several State societies are doing a great work in conducting inquiries on an extensive scale. Several normal schools and colleges have been enlisted, and progressive teachers in all classes of schools, together with thousands of mothers, have assisted the investigators by noting and reporting a multitude of facts about the life of the child as it comes into the world and grows into youth and manhood. These observations cover the development of the senses, the growth of perception and of the other mental activities, the awakening of the moral sense; the emotions, the occupations, the language, the ambitions of children; the ideas which children have of their rights, of their duties to each other, of punishment, of natural phenomena, of God; the influence of environment, together with many other subjects entering into the physical and mental history of the child.

So startling have been the results of these investigations that they are already forcing a restatement of several pedagogical principles and a general readjustment of school work and methods, particularly in the primary and intermediate grades. They are also greatly modifying the training of the children in many homes and are quickening the teachers to increased activity and to an interest in the child, which promises great things in the near future.

The principal aim of this book has been to bring the subject within the comprehension of the average teacher and parent. Technical terms and scientific formulæ have been avoided as much as possible. The desire to announce new principles has been wholly subservient to that of wishing to serve my fellow-workers by assisting them to a closer relationship with the child. One has well said, " It is strange that the child should be the last of all God's creatures to be studied scientifically." It is still more strange, however, that we have been content to teach children so long without knowing more about them as individuals. In explaining the work of a certain church, a lady said, " It's folks we're after, not things," and it is high time that we get after the child as much as after the things we teach him.

No time has been spent on anatomical descriptions; they can easily be found in current textbooks on physiology. Teachers and parents generally think it extremely difficult to pursue the study

of the child without at least a fair understanding
of the elements of psychology. They often forget
that the study will give them that very knowledge
and that, properly pursued, it is the best possible
introduction to psychology in general. So many
of the outlines and syllabi submitted for their guidance presuppose such knowledge that few under-
take to follow them. Every chapter in this book
is an attempt to organize the knowledge already
possessed by those who know little or nothing of
scientific psychology, and to assist them to inquiries which will give a clearer apprehension of
the nature and possibilities of the child.

Much child study, so called, has been done in
such an aimless, fragmentary way that its results
have been discouraging to some of its best friends.
If these pages assist in dignifying and systematiz-
ing the study, the author will be amply repaid.

Little claim is made to originality in the following chapters. Many of the books and periodicals named in the bibliography have served me in
greater or less degree, and I cheerfully acknowledge
my obligations to the authors for whatever of merit
may appear. A reasonable proportion of whatever
there may be of the opposite character the kind
reader will also charge to them.

I wish also to acknowledge my obligations to
several members of the faculty of the State Normal School for helpful suggestions.

A. R. TAYLOR.

STATE NORMAL SCHOOL, EMPORIA, KANSAS,
June 1, 1898.

Hilda and Josephine grew into womanhood as fast friends. Hilda married a poor but honest carpenter, and Josephine married a man of large estates who builded her a princely house. He took her to Europe and they visited all the great cities that she might purchase rare treasures for its furnishings. When all was put in place at home, Josephine sent for Hilda and showed her through every room. But as often as she finished explaining the figures on the carpets, the graceful folds of the draperies, the rich carvings of the furniture, the meanings of the pictures and the statuary that the masters had painted and chiseled, Hilda would say with a smile, "It is indeed beautiful, but there is something more beautiful than that." In disappointment, Josephine asked, "Hilda, what could be more beautiful?" Hilda slipped her arm into Josephine's, as of old, and said, "Come with me." They soon reached Hilda's humble home, with its plain but scrupulously clean white walls and doors. Little finger marks were seen on the door frame as they entered and a glad laugh greeted them from a ruddy-faced babe in the cradle. Hilda turned and said, "Josephine, there is nothing in all your grand home so beautiful as those finger marks on the door and the merry prattle of my sweet babe!" Tears started to Josephine's eyes as she folded her friend to her breast and said, "Hilda, you are right."—After Eugene Field.

xix

CONTENTS.

ANALYSIS OF CONTENTS.

xxviTHE STUDY OF THE CHILD.

50. Its intellectual value.
51. The knowledge given by the purely visual function of the eye.
52. The union of the visual and muscular sensations.
53. Dependence of sight upon touch—symbolism.
54. The æsthetic value of sight.
55. The care of the eye—diseases and tests.

Chapter VIII, pages 54 to 59.

GENERAL FUNCTIONS OF THE SENSES.

56. The means of communicating with the external world.
57. The action of the sensory nerves.
58. The dependence of the mind upon the delicacy of the senses.
59. The *sensation continuum*.
60. Relative prominence of sensations in the life of the child and adult.
61. How the senses are cultivated.

Chapter IX, pages 60 to 68.

CONSCIOUSNESS AND APPERCEPTION.

62. The bridge from the physical to the mental.
63. How sensations come into consciousness.
64. The rise of the idea of identity and difference.
65. The process of apperception.
66. How knowledge and experience organize a child.
67. The law of apperception.
68. The law of association.

Chapter XIII, pages 93 to 105.

MUSCULAR OR MOTOR CONTROL.

Chapter XIV, pages 106 to 114.

THE FEELINGS.

Chapter XV, pages 115 to 123.

THE WILL AND ITS FUNCTIONS.

3

Chapter XX, pages 168 to 178.

MANNERS AND MORALS.

Chapter XXI, pages 179 to 194.

NORMALS AND ABNORMALS.

Chapter XXII, pages 195 to 207.

STAGES OF GROWTH, FATIGUE POINT, ETC.

Chapter XXIII, pages 208 to 210.

CONCLUSIONS.

INTRODUCTORY.

IF asked for the name of that which is at once most like and most unlike God, almost any one would answer, *The babe in the cradle.* In it are all the attributes of God, but they are there *in potentia* only. They are there in kind, but in the least quantity that can possibly exist. God has the same attributes, but in quantity limitless, in knowledge boundless, in majesty supreme. Between these two extremes are men in all stages of development. If we represent the progress or the growth of the child toward God by a triangle, we shall find the babe at the apex, *b*, the youth slightly out on the base line at *y*, and the growing man

at different stages, *m*, *m'*, *m''*, *m'''*, beyond, in varying development up toward God standing at the other end of the base and filling the triangle at an infinite distance away. How near the apex some men remain! How far on toward God some men advance! Who knows just where stand Moses

and Plato and Paul and Bacon and Milton and
Kepler and Newton and Knox and Mozart and
Wesley, and all that mighty host of men who
walked amid the stars and dared to think God's
thoughts after him? On, on to the right, away
beyond the ken of ordinary mortals, they are still
advancing in wisdom and power that one day, it
is said reverently, shall make them approach even
to God himself.

Here lies in my hand a young bird; all it can
be, all it can do, may now be written at once by
any one. Who dare say what that babe lying in
yonder cradle shall be and do? Who is able to
place a limit upon the result of its efforts at reaching up toward the Infinite?

Various attempts have been made to state the
object of education. Plato would have it to be the
perfection of all the powers of man. Dante de-
clared it to be to fit man for eternity. Milton
thought it to be to regain what man lost in
Adam's fall.. Spencer says that it is to prepare
man for complete living. Rosenkranz makes the
object to be to develop the theoretical and practical
reason in man, to give him freedom. Few, however, seem to emphasize fully the idea that its end
is to advance the youth in his efforts to become
like the Infinite. In his image is he created, and
every activity exerted should be a striving to realize the possibilities thus assured.

Much has been written upon the sacredness of
the child and the great responsibility resting upon
parent and teacher; but however keenly any one
may have felt it all, there come a weightier sig-

nificance and a deeper meaning as this higher end of education becomes more clear. He no longer teaches geography and arithmetic as an end but as a means. He no longer finds satisfaction in discovering that his children know all about trade winds and simooms, about Aristides and George Washington, about the Faerie Queene and Evangeline, but rather in discovering that their minds are growing in power to think and that they are enlarging in grasp and vision with each day's efforts.

In studying the child, we are in reality studying the man. In studying it, we are enabled to see the steps by which the material becomes spiritual, blind physical impulse becomes unerring skill, the finite becomes the infinite. The proper study of mankind is man, but he who knows not the child will never know the man.

All other sciences center around the science of the child, for there is no other which does not contribute in some way to our understanding of him. Those upon which we must depend most directly are, of course, anatomy, physiology, and hygiene, with all their various subdivisions; ethics, logic, and psychology, including their genetic and practical phases. It was out of the study of man that these sciences came, and on that account they are valuable as guides to the study of the child.

No one can profitably engage in child study without children to study—not one child only, but many children. Some valuable contributions to the subject have been made by those who have devoted their time to the study of one child, but only as the results of a large number of such investigations are collated can any reliable inferences be drawn. Reading about children is not studying children, and little good will come of it. They must be studied in their homes, in their plays, in the schoolroom, at their work, at their books, asleep, awake, alone, with their inferiors and their superiors, in moments of despondency and in moments of triumph, wherever they may reveal themselves to us and wherever we may be able to gain admittance to their real selves. Some children will be found apt, wide-awake, aggressive; others slow, sluggish, passive. Some have perfect physical organisms, others defective eyesight or hearing, or possibly a growing deformity in limb or body. Some imitate instantly, others have little motor control. Some are as lovable as angels; others vicious to an extreme. Some will be found simple and natural; others artificial and affected; some tractable, others unmanageable.

But these discoveries are worth nothing, if the study of the children ends here. A physician is of no value if he stops when he has taken the diagnosis of a case. He must now proceed with the application of a remedy, a process that requires even greater skill. So the student of the child must immediately set about to discover the most economic means and methods of correcting the defects in the child and of stimulating its normal activities. All these investigations should result in giving us an idea of what constitutes a normal child and in helping to understand the laws of his development. Many people are as exacting in their demands of the child as they are of a full-grown man or woman, forgetting absolutely the great difference between the two—physically, mentally, and morally. It is of vital importance that we know what we may expect of the child. Nearly as many children are ruined by the unreasonable demands made upon them as by the neglect sadly too common. How quickly and generously do the flowers respond to the tender, intelligent touch of the housewife—and yet even more generously does the child respond to the solicitations of one who knows its impulses and sympathizes with its every need.

Much of value will be found in recalling one's childhood and the experiences and impressions of those days when the heart was young and the mind was thrilling at its first acquaintance with things that long since have been regarded as commonplace and insignificant. This process helps us to put ourselves in the place of the child, and to think and feel as he thinks and feels. Memory may not be very clear on many points, but what does reappear brings us much nearer to the child than we were before.

Caution should always be observed and hasty generalizations avoided. One swallow does not make a summer, neither does one observation establish a law. The slightest change in conditions has overthrown many a finely spun theory. We are dealing with the mind, not with physical forces. The most sensitive instrument ever invented by man does not compare with it in delicacy. The impulses that direct its activities come from depths that no plummet has yet fathomed, and progress must necessarily be slow.

Do not forget that the study you are asked to make is not necessarily for the purpose of contributing the results to the profession in general, but rather for the particular benefit of your particular children and of yourself as their teacher. Your enlightenment and their advancement are more important than anything else. Let love and interest in them and in them alone prompt you in it all.

Child study generally begins with the babe's first conscious movements, though an exhaustive treatment of the subject would include its prenatal life as well. Those of our readers who may care to know more of the various views of the genesis of certain physical and mental activities would do well to consult Perez's First Three Years of Childhood, Preyer's The Senses and the Will, and Compayré's Intellectual and Moral Development of the Child.

The mystery of conscious life, both in its origin and development, confronts us at the very beginning of the study. No other phenomenon in the universe approaches it in sublimity, no other so fascinates us by its delicate subtleness. The force of gravitation that holds the stars in their courses, the fervent heat that melts down mountains and tosses them into the sky, the bolt of lightning that shivers the towering monarchs of the forest, powerful though they be, know not themselves nor direct a single one of their myriad activities. That strange and wonderful attribute, conscious life, is reserved for the child, the man. It sits ruler and king over every activity of the soul and over the mighty forces that hitherto have recognized no master save their Creator.

As the senses awaken the child into this conscious life, they are treated in the opening chapters.

THE STUDY OF THE CHILD.

CHAPTER I.

THE SENSES.—ORGANIC.

It is through the senses that the child wakes to conscious life, through them that he becomes acquainted with the outer world, which he is to know and of which he is to become a counterpart. Without them the child lies dormant in his cradle, sleeping away his days, not even knowing of an outer world, nor dreaming of his own mighty possibilities. With his senses he explores the universe round about him and eventually becomes its master. Upon their sensitiveness and perfection his progress depends. No greater joy comes to a new mother than the assurance that the child has a perfect body and perfect eyes and ears, but it is seldom that she recognizes the full significance of such a boon. Those eyes and ears are not only to enable him to place himself in space and communicate with his fellows, but to furnish him the materials, the food upon which his mind is to feed and grow. They are not only to give him a knowledge of the sensuous world round about him, but also of those higher relations and harmonies that knit soul with soul and with the Infinite.

It is important that mother and teacher know at once the tremendous significance of any physical defect, particularly as it may in any way pertain to the nervous system of the child. Whatever disturbs or obstructs, however slightly, the natural and spontaneous movement of the sensor or motor activities may have a vast influence in shaping the intellectual life and the moral character of the child. *Two seemingly parallel straight lines may be but an inch apart at their origin and yet be ten feet apart at the end of a mile.* Intellectual dullness and moral obliquity are usually due to some physical deformity, though often so insignificant as to escape notice.

Some time since, twenty bad boys in a certain city were chosen for the sense test, and it was discovered that every one of them was defective in vision or hearing, or both. Twenty good children were selected, and it happened that all were perfect in both senses. It would be dangerous to generalize from this that all physical defectives are morally defective, or that all perfect nervous systems are morally without reproach, but that the tendency of each is here emphasized there can be no question. A sound mind in a sound body means more than that the body should be healthy; it means that every part of the physical organism should be continuously and efficiently performing its proper function. There are notable cases of individuals, physically defective from birth, attaining to great mental power and spiritual excellence, but at what cost few people can imagine.

Though derangement may not clearly manifest itself in the young child, its presence may often be detected by an expert and corrected by judicious treatment. Many an eye that was weak at birth has been put out by ignorant or careless nurses; many an ear that scarce had taken form has been ruined by those who loved the child best. Many a child has lost one sense or both through the neglect of ignorance or caprice. On the other hand, physicians tell us that one half of the children with defective hearing can easily be cured, if taken in time; the same is true of those defective in eyesight. Is this, then, a light theme to which we are giving attention?

It does not seem wise to spend much time in discussing the lower senses, for they give us little knowledge, comparatively speaking. And yet they are of the highest importance. All those sensations which may be embraced under the one term, *organic,* such as the feelings arising from the general state of the body or of the vital and vegetative organs, make up the tone of the body as a whole and give it that peculiar physical character which manifests itself in what is known as the temperament of the individual. The general disposition of the child is so largely determined by the degree of perfection with which the digestive, assimilative, circulatory, respiratory, and lymphatic functions are performed, that no student of the child can afford to overlook them. The old notion that the bile exercises a controlling influence over the disposition of the individual is simply expanded in

these days to embrace all the forces named above.
That a child whose stomach is souring and effeves-
cing half the day should be amiable and attentive
to his work, can not be expected; that one whose
circulation is heavy and sluggish should naturally
be apt and quick in perception and response, is out
of harmony with all experience; that one whose
physical condition is never animated nor buoyant,
can without effort be cheerful and aggressive, is one
of the things few thoughtful people believe. And
yet, in spite of all this, we are almost continually
overlooking the physical cause of children's temperaments and dispositions; and seeking to correct
them by scolding, punishing, and other traditional
and irrational remedies. Often a child has been
whipped for failing to complete work assigned in
an allotted time, when the effort required would
have completely prostrated him; he has been boxed
for restlessness, when one good, wholesome meal
would have appeased a hunger that would not let
him be still; he has been ridiculed for melancholy
that diet and exercise only could drive away; he
has been degraded for failing to prepare a lesson,
when headache or indigestion was wholly responsible. Fretfulness, restlessness, *ennui*, indifference, stupidity, willfulness, timidity, nervousness,
impulsiveness, and many kindred mental maladies
in children that perplex and annoy and defeat the
teacher and parent are the natural products of
disorders in digestion, circulation, or some other
purely physiological function. It is nothing less
than a crime for any one to ignore the real cause
of such manifestations in the child and to attempt

to correct them by reproof and punishment. Such treatment only aggravates the trouble, soon making it chronic, whereas a rational treatment would generally give permanent physical relief and then the mental distemper would easily yield, often even disappearing of its own accord. There are few full-grown men and women of such equable temperaments that they are not more or less disturbed by similar causes. If this be the case with those whose wills have been trained through a course of years, how much more it must be true of children whose every action is dictated so largely by physical impulses.

These facts need neither elaboration nor illustration; but they do need repetition and emphasis. Many a child has been roughly shaken for crying, when a pin was later discovered to be the cause of the trouble. Others have been dosed and drugged for peevishness that was caused by thirst only. Others, again, have been jolted on a friendly but a villainously mistaken knee for screaming, when every jolt but intensified the awful pain with which colic was already stabbing the child. Thus blindly do we attempt to relieve and correct the physical and mental ills of the babe. Do we approach it with more wisdom when it is five years of age? If the healthy action of these various organic functions is so important in the formation of the child's temperament and disposition, then a thorough theoretical and practical knowledge of food principles, of hygiene, of symptoms and remedies, of the structure, development, and function of every organ of

the body, as well as of the relations of all these
to the psychical activities, is little enough to
demand of every mother. That such knowledge
is uncommon makes the need of it the more common.

CHAPTER II.

THE SENSES (CONTINUED).—TEMPERATURE.

THE organic senses just mentioned embrace those senses not so clearly differentiated in the consciousness as the six senses generally recognized. They give us a knowledge of muscular movement, of hunger and thirst, of fatigue, of respiration, of disease, feelings of relish, of depression, of exhilaration, etc. Few of them are localized. They pertain rather to the system as a whole than to any particular part of it.

The sense of temperature is now clearly distinguished from the sense of touch and really makes the seventh sense, if those above mentioned are still embraced in the term organic. Take a toothpick or a sharp-pointed lead pencil and touch various parts of the palm of the hand and it will sometimes appear warm and sometimes cold, with occasional places where neither effect appears. By the use of delicate instruments the presence and location of these warm, cold, and neutral spots have been definitely determined and mapped. It would appear that certain nerve filaments have special temperature functions entirely distinct from those of touch. That the warm and cold spots are more numerous and more sensitive in

7

some people than in others is readily seen in the
ease with which some people handle hot bars, hot
plates, etc., or with which they put their hands or
feet into hot water, or drink hot liquids, while
others are almost thrown into spasms when they
attempt it. The character of the epidermis—the
outer skin—has much to do with the sensitiveness
to heat or cold. The calloused hand of a blacksmith or a cook enables him to handle hot pokers
and stove lids that would blister the tender fingers
of a child. A mother not infrequently scalds the
feet of her child by forcing them into water which
is " hardly warm " to her toughened fingers, and
so brings on disorders far more serious than that
which she was striving to cure. Many a babe's
mouth is sorely blistered by a hot gargle that the
nurse, accustomed to drink boiling-hot tea three
times a day, declares to be " just warm, now
dearie." Hot plasters and poultices are clapped
on the little innocents without intelligence or
mercy for the same reasons, and incalculable injury is thus done to a multitude of children.

Incidentally, it should here be mentioned that
some children are naturally warmer-blooded and
need less clothing than others; they are often suffering from the heat in a room where others are
perfectly comfortable. They need food with more
nitrogenous and less fatty material in it than their
colder-blooded fellows. I had a neighbor whose
veins were always surcharged with rich blood, who
kept his home four or five degrees cooler in winter than the normal, 68° to 70°, and his children
with thinner blood were constantly suffering more

or less in consequence. Another, with sluggish arteries, kept his home so warm that his boys and girls, inheriting their mother's vigorous temperament, were often nervously prostrate. They took cold nearly everywhere they went, and certain serious ills were surely chargeable to nothing else.

If this were strictly a mother's book, I would enter into details concerning a variety of skin diseases in which the temperature sense is more or less involved, and which contribute their full share toward the development of the disposition of the child, but I shall content myself with a mere reference to them and with a reminder that there are far higher reasons for getting rid of them promptly than merely for the sake of the comfort and health of the child.

Sufficient has been said, however, to show the teacher the necessity of studying the temperature problem as applied to every child in his classes. It is impossible to have an equable temperature in every part of a room, particularly when heated by a stove, but it is possible to put the colder-blooded and the thinly clad near the stove and the others in more distant parts of the room. It is also possible to manage the heat so as to keep it near the normal. The health of the children requires it; comfort, good order, and effective instruction are impossible without it. Friendly feeling and interest in work seldom develop in a cold room; reflective thought and keen analysis are paralyzed in a hot one. Many teachers owe their failure in keeping order to inability to keep the schoolroom properly ventilated and heated.

The test for the normal temperature of a child is possibly best made by conferring with the mother, and by a few inquiries of the child himself from day to day. Thermometers applied to the body will be of little avail. It will take but a week or two for a teacher to discover whether a pupil is above or below the average normal and to seat him accordingly. Of course, he should not make the mistake of thinking that temperature alone must decide the question of location. Some children are very sensitive to draughts, while others seem to be affected little by them. The seeds of permanent ill health or of fatal disease may easily be given root in a single day by neglecting these precautions.

Two seemingly parallel straight lines may be but an inch apart at their origin and yet be ten feet apart at the end of a mile. So these little things may not seem of much moment at present, but in a few years their effect is too sadly realized.

The intellectual value of the senses thus far mentioned is very small. They simply give us a knowledge of the condition of the physical organism in a general and in a specific way; some of them not even localizing a disorder or a want of the body—as thirst, hunger, etc. The temperature sense is easily recognized as one step higher in the series, for it not only gives us a knowledge of the general temperature of the body, but of individual parts of the body as well. Further, it is the first to give us a knowledge of the external world, but even that knowledge is limited to the simple information concerning its temperature as compared with that of the body. While the others permit a child to say, " I am hungry, I am tired, I feel my hand moving, I have the colic, I am sick at the stomach," this sense permits him to say, " I am cold," and to add, " It is cold," meaning something *outside of himself,* as the air, a chair, water, the bed, the poker, etc.

The organic senses give him immediate knowledge of his physical well- or ill-being only, while his skill in many of the arts is dependent in large measure upon the delicacy with which he discriminates temperature. The thermometer serves a useful purpose in many of them, but if the artisan relies upon it alone he will be a poor workman indeed. The need, then, of great care in cultivating this sense for the sake of bodily comfort and bodily health is almost equaled by the practical demands made in everyday life. Few more helpless creatures can be imagined than those who have lost the sense by which they appreciate heat or cold, and so are liable to sustain frightful injury without being conscious of it until it is revealed by some other sense. So, in a practical way, how sorry a laundress is the girl who has not learned how to test the temperature of her sadiron, or how provoking is a cook who is unable to discover the right temperature of her oven by a single sweep of her hand, how culpable is a housekeeper or a teacher if she lack in ability to notice the changes in the temperature of the rooms in which the children live. A part, then, of every child's education is to learn how to use this sense skillfully and profitably.

CHAPTER III.

Possibly the first sense to begin differentiating is that of taste. The first food entering the mouth not only satisfies hunger, but is grateful to the taste as well. It may be that the newborn child is provided with taste buds that respond even more generously than they do later, for the specific purpose of encouraging it to take the food Nature has provided. At any rate, a very short time suffices to enable it to discriminate between the sweet and wholesome milk and the insipid or adulterated article, as many nurses can fully testify. From such a simple beginning, skill in distinguishing among foods grows until many thousand different kinds can easily be detected. So highly may this sense be educated that it is said that expert tea tasters in the employ of the great tea houses can easily recognize as high as fifty different kinds of teas that have been mixed and steeped together. Epicures and lovers of the table in general are not necessarily gormands and gluttons, for they find their highest enjoyment not in the amount they eat, but rather in its ability to awaken pleasurable taste. Ten times more labor is put upon foods and drinks to make them pala-

12

table than is put upon them to make them wholesome. Nine cooks out of ten work to tickle the
palate more than to insure ready digestion. The
" best " things at the average table are those that
awaken a new and pleasing sensation at the time
of eating, rather than comfort afterward. Even
the staples come to the table with subtle flavors
that the ingenuity of the cook has dexterously
added. Fruits in incredible variety are cultivated,
not so much for their nutritive quality as for their
ability to awaken corresponding variety in relish.
The forests of the earth are searched for nuts and
oils and leaves and roots that may stimulate a
wider range of pleasure in the mouth of man.
Luxuries, those dishes that delight the palate but
serve little as tissue builders, cost us more money
than the necessaries of life. Many men are kept
poor to the end of their days because most of their
earnings go into this red-hot hopper! More sickness and physical misery are caused by eating
highly seasoned food than by any dozen other
causes combined. That which Nature designed as
a gentle stimulus to taste and to digestion has
too generally become the scourge to both. Nature
intended that taste and digestion should be warm
friends: we have often made them bitter enemies.
Then, for purely physical reasons, the proper cultivation of the sense of taste assumes proportions
in the care and culture of the child that few people understand. It is just as important as exercise or sleep.

Parents insist on their children eating slowly
and chewing their food well, but, while that is es-

sential, there are other weighty things in the law
also. When they are apprehended, they will read
somewhat as follows:

For the first dozen years of a child's life his
sense of taste should be developed with the same
care as the control and use of his voluntary muscles
or of any of the organs of the body. Highly seasoned foods and stimulating drinks should seldom
be given him. On the contrary, wholesome food
in sufficient variety of kind and flavor should be
given to make eating a pleasure and to maintain
easy digestion and healthy growth. Children's
appetites are the best spices at any table. If they
be wanting, it is poor economy to resort to artificial means. It frequently happens that a child
refuses every dish on the table and clamors for
one that his rugged father finds it difficult to
digest. It is better that he eat nothing until the
next meal than to yield to his appeal. A month's
indulgence in such demands often insures dys-
pepsia before the child is twenty years of age.
Of course, it is as cruel and unreasonable to force
children to eat things for which they have an aversion, as it would be to force them to look at colors
that pain the eye. With very few resources and
very little tact any mother may easily discover
what suitable dishes her children like and provide
them in sufficient variety to make every meal a
delight. Simple foods satisfy children, and the
change should come in variety and not in sea-
soning.

This is not the place to enter into the discussion of the subject of the preparation of food, but

it should be said that the art of cooking is being revolutionized in these days, and that what a poor cook has been covering up with sugar and salt and pepper and spices, the new cook is presenting in both a palatable and a digestible form with the merest suggestion of the spice box. All hail to the new system, but it has a great work yet to do in solving the problem for the normal development of the sense of taste in the child. With that under proper control, the health problem solves more easily.

The sense of taste is not to be cultivated by suppressing and confining it to a few foods. The greater the number and variety of the simpler forms, Nature's own productions, the less demand will there be for foods of the hot tamale order. But even here great harm may be done in nurturing a desire for change that may react, begetting disorders similar to those just mentioned. The intimate relationship between the mind and the vegetative system is so close that the former can never be ignored in considering the food problem. Imagination and emotion powerfully affect both taste and digestion. The course to be pursued in the case of each individual child can only be determined as his tastes, already awakening, are discovered and the resources of his family are known. Then the problem for the mother is not to find ways and means for pandering to them, but for correcting and educating them. Lectures may do them little good, but the right kind of dishes will sooner or later accomplish the end.

Not only is all this to be done for the sake of

the health of the child, but for his moral character as well. Taste for highly seasoned food and
stimulating drinks almost invariably becomes appetite, consuming and uncontrollable, later in life.
Its long train of evils need not be rehearsed here.
No heart is so pure, no soul so noble, that physical appetite long unrestrained does not corrupt.
Every mother has it in her power to *form* the
tastes and appetites of her children. They are
always *formed*, but the process of *re-*forming is
frequently a heartbreaking failure. Crimes hide-
ous and revolting might easily have been prevented
by a little intelligence and firmness in shaping the
tastes of the child for food and drink. Nothing
ever written is truer than this.

This sense is also intended to contribute to
man's physical enjoyment. Its proper cultivation
refines and enlarges that enjoyment not only in
a sensuous way, but in an intellectual way as well.
So intimately is the delicate discrimination of
foods allied to good judgment in an intellectual,
and particularly in an æsthetic way, that the
word taste is universally used in distinguishing
men and women of refined culture from those of
the commoner sort.

The sense of taste is used in many of the arts
and sciences, though possibly not so generally as
that of smell and the others to be mentioned here-
after. Every good cook—and half of the human
race ought to be good cooks—needs a highly cultivated taste to test the quality of her mixtures and
dishes; she is helpless without it. The mineralogist, the grocer, the pharmacist, the physician, the

fruit dealer, the confectioner, the dairyman, the
restaurateur, the baker, and many other professional, industrial, and commercial people find
highly developed taste invaluable. A great army
of men and women are employed in the preparation and sale of foods. The excellence of every
pound prepared or sold is dependent upon the degree of cultivation of the taste of manufacturer
and tradesman. Everywhere you turn you easily
see the practical value of an educated taste.

CHAPTER IV.

THE SENSES (CONTINUED).—SMELL.

IN the order of intellectual value the sense of smell is next to be noted. It also serves a double function, subjective and objective. For some time after birth it is not differentiated from the other physical senses, but at about the age of three months begins to serve as a help in distinguishing food and soon after to contribute materially to the sensuous pleasures of the child. With taste, it stands a watchful guardian to protect the system from injurious foods. It also adds much to the relish of many dishes by mingling the enjoyment of their aroma with that of their flavor. The grateful feeling throughout the whole body accompanying slight changes in temperature serves well as an introduction to the higher physical pleasures that fragrant odors produce. Poets sing of the delights of the bath and of the gentle zephyrs that lull to restful sleep, but their lyres assume a lighter, quicker movement as they describe the odors of the

"May-flowers blooming around them ;
Fragrant, filling the air with a strange and wonderful sweetness."

18

For the physical well-being alone, the organ
of smell needs that same careful attention that
any other sense organ demands. Its structure is
easily understood by reference to any work on
anatomy or physiology. The delicacy of the
Schneiderian membrane, on which are spread out
the fine filaments of the olfactory nerve and
against which the odorous particles must pass, is,
however, not so generally appreciated as it ought
to be. The turbinated chambers are kept pliable
and sensitive by a regular supply of moisture
whose slight variation affects at once both the
ability to distinguish odors and the health of the
organ. Probably no other organ so quickly reveals a great variety of bodily disorders. It serves
as a distress flag, giving notice of internal derangement. It is liable to painful diseases of its own,
such as catarrh, polypi. adenoidal growths, etc.
Most of them are more incident to childhood than
to manhood, and unless promptly detected and
suppressed become the generators of a whole brood
of ills that make life miserable for one's companions as well as for himself. Sometimes the'
trouble originates in one duct, sometimes in both.
It frequently happens that the sense of smell in a
child is practically destroyed, and that an offensive
disease has fastened itself upon him before the
parents know that anything is wrong. No child
ever has a cold, or a fever, or frontal inflamma-
tions of any character, that may not settle in that
tender network of bone and nerves at the base of
the nose. Skin eruptions are likely to find a home
there also. Occasionally some insect or some hard

substance lodges in one of the canals and endangers even the life of the child. The only safe course with children is to be constantly on the lookout for disorders. Sympathetic intimacy with them will usually bring them to you on the slightest disturbance in this or in any other organ, and their appeal should have instant and intelligent response. The derangement may not seem serious and it may be but temporary. If it be serious, however, or if it does not appear serious and yet is persistent, medical assistance should be sought. Often these nasal affections are manifestations of systemic disturbances, but, whether one or the other, remedies can not too quickly be applied.

Two seemingly parallel straight lines may be but an inch apart at their origin and yet be ten feet apart at the end of a mile, and a nasal disorder that appears very slight in the child may in manhood be robbing life of all its pleasure.

This little volume would grow to undue proportions if space should be taken to describe the diseases to which the different sense organs are subject, together with their symptoms and remedies, and yet the object would not be attained if simple methods of discovering the affections were not presented. The closing of one nostril by external pressure with the finger and the child's effort to force air through the other as he expels it from the lungs readily reveals obstructions and frequently removes them. The inability of the child to breathe through his nostrils, which is the way Nature intended, is always cause for attention, though in case of colds not necessarily for uneasiness. If a child of six or seven has no cold, and yet can not distinguish the odors of flowers, perfumes, kinds of fruit, etc., the cause of it should be ascertained as soon as possible and its removal intelligently attempted. Very simple remedies may prove effectual at once. Possibly the development of this sense is a little belated and the presentation of a few strikingly different odors may at once arouse and stimulate it. If the child complains of dull pains or of pressure between the eyes for a week or two, it is a sure sign of incipient catarrh, or of a kindred disease, and needs skillful treatment.

To the general feeling of well-being, when the other senses already mentioned are responding naturally, the sense of temperature may possibly add the slightest glimmer of the æsthetic element, but it comes into grateful prominence with the growth of the sense of smell. In addition to its utility as a factor in determining the nature of food, smell also proves of great value in an intellectual and practical way. It assists in getting knowledge of a thousand things in the world round about us. The botanist is dependent upon it for distinguishing many varieties of plants; the mineralogist would be sorely handicapped in classifying minerals if his sense of smell were to fail him; the biologist without a good nose would be almost as bad as a miner without a lantern; the chemist would be in greater confusion than Pandora, when she opened her famous box, if he were unable to discover the odor of the various compounds in his laboratory. What is true of the sciences is also as true of the arts.

Many diseases are revealed to the physician largely by their odor. The plumber and gasfitter would not earn his salt who could not discover the presence of deleterious or poisonous gases by their peculiar odor. Without this sense the cook could hardly know that a stew is burning, a sauce is fermenting, an egg is addled, or that a dish will prove relishable at the table. Without this sense one would succeed poorly in handling drugs, perfumery, groceries, farm products of all kinds, etc. Without it what would become of

> "The butcher and the baker
> And the candlestick maker?"

Properly trained, it is a good insurance against fire, for it often reveals the presence of fire in the house long before any other sense discovers it.

The sense of smell as an æsthetic sense has already been mentioned. It has always been prized, even among barbarous nations, for its pleasure-producing capacities; the sweet-smelling unguent and the musk-scented ointment are as popular among the wild men of Borneo as among the *dilettante* of the salons of Paris. Fragrant odors vied with the cithara and the harp in the entertainments at the royal palaces of Egypt, of Assyria, of Phœnicia, of Greece, and of Rome. As guests entered, the glad welcome of sweet music was even excelled by the sweeter perfumes, whose fragrance filled the ambient air; the rich tapestries, the multicolored rugs, the luxurious couches exhaled the attar of roses, the aroma of myrrh and of the pomegranate; while fine spray, laden with lavender, fell in floating mists over the fair company as they passed around and among the rare plants that added their wealth of beauty to the splendor of the scene. Gentle ladies through all the ages have sought the choicest waters and perfumes for their toilets, and they are now regarded as necessaries in the boudoir of every cultivated woman, whether Christian or pagan. But however successfully art may bring captive these rare extracts from Nature's rarest laboratories, the perfumed air of springtime, of summer, and of autumn gray, freighted with the blushes of opening flowers, with the rustle of nodding grain, and the aroma of the mellowing fruit, awakens harmonies and images of subtler beauty and deeper meaning.

But much of this is known to everybody, and it finds a place here simply to emphasize more fully the importance of the care and culture of the sense of smell. The noseless man knows less by far than many people imagine. Into whatever walk or occupation in life a child is to go, he will need for his physical well-being, for his general knowledge, for his æsthetic enjoyment, for his practical use, a sensitive, delicately discriminating sense of smell. The health of the organ is the first requisite, but that is important only as enabling it to profit by training and to attain unto the highest possible perfection. The means at hand are so various and so abundant that further suggestions will be withheld until the chapter on general methods of cultivating the senses is reached.

CHAPTER V.

THE SENSES (CONTINUED).—TOUCH.

THE child enters the world furnished with all the instruments necessary for becoming acquainted with it, for protecting itself against it, and for finally becoming its master. Nature kindly anticipated the coming by providing the child with a more or less perfect covering, so that the shock of transition shall not be too great. In spite of this fact, it frequently happens that even a slight change of temperature or the contact with its clothing, though ever so soft, produces great pain. What effect the manner of handling the child in these first few hours or days has upon its future life, the Infinite only knows; but that it has a right to intelligent, sympathetic care, none but a brute denies. Nature still remains its friend, and slowly hardens the epidermal cells, so that soon the extreme sensitiveness is gone and the child rests quietly in its crib. The delicate terminal nerve filaments that at first were easily set on fire are covered a little more fully, and all over the body companion filaments begin to respond in an orderly, pleasurable way to outside pressure.

Through the sensations thus aroused the child

24

soon begins an acquaintance with the external world and succeeds in localizing, or placing, at least in a general way, the objects touching it. What a wonderful thousand-direction sense is this sense of touch! As the babe lies in the cradle, nothing can come in contact with it on back or front, on hand or foot, above or below, right or left, but that the news is instantly carried to the brain. If the object be rough or sharp, irritation results; if it be soft or smooth, gratification.

The sense of touch increases in sensitiveness and delicacy much more rapidly in some parts of the body than in others. If two toothpicks, or pencils, or a pair of dividers be separated slightly at the points and lightly pressed against the cheek of a child, he will probably declare that there is but one point touching him, but if applied to the lips, tip of the tongue, or finger, he will immediately say there are two. If now the distance between the points be increased and applied again to the cheek, he may detect two points, but on being applied to the neck, only one. The thigh is found to possess less power of discrimination than any other part of the body; the fingers and the tongue tip the greatest. This difference in discrimination is due to the difference in the distances between the various nerve endings of the sense of touch. One great peculiarity about them is that they seem to multiply with use. There are also differences in what is called the threshold value of touch—that is, the degree of pressure required to awaken sensation. This also varies in different parts of the body and in different persons.

The offices of this sense in the physical economy are easily seen to be various. It is essential to the protection of all parts of the body against injury, and, like the sense of temperature, is more sensitive in parts that are most susceptible to harm. It immediately reveals the presence of insects and vermin of every description; of objects in the way or coming against it, whether sharp or dull, rough or smooth, hard or soft; and of too great pressure or constriction of any part of the clothing. Through association, it indirectly reveals much concerning such objects that is not given by pressure proper. What miserable creatures we should be if compelled to wait for a fly to bite or a mosquito to fill his nib before knowing of his presence. Think of the suffering which would everywhere ensue if we could know nothing of a rough substance until continual rubbing against it had produced rawness or inflammation of the skin. The sense of touch is the special guardian of the eye. Whenever it fails in its duty there, intense suffering may result. It also prevents the ears and mouth and nose from many a sad mishap. Contact with the tongue often reveals the nature of food by association before the sense of taste has been aroused, and, so together with smell, touch assists taste to discriminate among foods and to protect the system against offensive or poisonous substances.

This *passive* touch is greatly re-enforced and multiplied by the addition of muscular movements and their associated sensations. It is then called *active* touch, because the voluntary muscles are

exercised in bringing any part of the body desired
into contact with an object. As an illustration,
the arm may be thrown around a column, the feet
run over a ball, the fingers clasped around an ink
bottle, the hand slipped rapidly over a book, and
in each case the varying pressure, combined with
the different muscular sensations, reveals the shape
and surface of the object. It is now conceded that
the idea of solidity itself, the idea of three dimen-
sions—length, breadth, and thickness—is derived
through active touch. Without it, every object
would appear flat and no adequate conception of
the positions of objects in space could be attained.
This co-operation of the muscles gives the touch a
sufficient number of simultaneous or of rapidly
successive sensations to enable the mind to determine the shape, size, surface, texture, and hardness
of an object. Much skill in discriminating, as
with the other senses, develops slowly and develops
with practice only. The time comes, however,
when the amount of muscular movement required
is very slight in any given case and by a process
of association and symbolism, to be explained later,
the mind instantly recognizes the characteristics
named. The distance from one part of an object
to another is revealed by the observed amount of
muscular effort required to move the hand or part
of the hand from one to the other. The distance
between objects is determined in the same way,
though other muscles may be used and other parts
of the body, or the whole body, moved, as in the
case of walking or jumping.

Though afterward, by association and symbolism, this special function of touch is largely assumed by sight, the accuracy of sight perception as well as of the information still furnished us by touch, is entirely dependent upon the way in which the sense of touch is educated in the child. This sense is sometimes defective or belated, and what is often ascribed to the dullness of the child's intellect or to inattention and indifference is found upon investigation to be due to one of the causes named. The test can easily be made by placing in the child's hand a variety of forms, surfaces, and textures for him to compare. He should not be tested on his ability to designate by the proper terms, for that tests his memory and not his physical sense, but upon his ability to pick out two or more things of similar shape, surface, or texture; in a similar way, by touch only, also to tell relative sizes of objects. If he be found lacking, the divider and pressure tests may also be used. It is highly probable that few cases will be found where daily exercises in discriminating by touch will not in a reasonable time show surprisingly happy results. Mere guesses should not be allowed. Accuracy, then rapidity, must be the constant aim. If, after a few weeks, no appreciable progress is discoverable, a physician should make an examination and advise upon the course to be pursued. The cause may not lie in the peripheral nor in the afferent nerves, but in the brain, and the sooner known the better. Possibly methods of educating the sense have been wrong; possibly general nervous derangement frustrates the efforts; possibly in some way the child's mind has not yet learned how to

treat the sensations that are constantly pouring
into his little soul, and some gentle means must be
used to make that connection between mind and
body which, in some way, failed at the critical moment when Nature intended it should be made.

The intellectual value of touch, the power to
give us knowledge of the external world, is seldom
placed high enough. Without the sense of touch
the child would not only see things flat, but the
myriad forms that fill the earth and sky would
never be known to him. All of them would be
alike to him—neither rough nor smooth, fine nor
coarse, sharp nor blunt, round nor square, far nor
near, in high nor low relief. In fact, he would
have no idea in the concrete or in the abstract of
any such qualities. He would, in manhood, be
tumbling downstairs, over chairs, into the fire-
place, into the washtub, and everywhere else, just
as he does in childhood before this sense has taught
him the relief and relations of objects. Without
it he would know neither sea nor land, wood nor
mineral. If man were deprived of the sense of
touch, every loom, every ship, every railway car,
every industry in which man is engaged, would
instantly stop. All these are dependent upon its
high cultivation for their successful conduct. No
matter for what occupation a child is intended,
the education of this sense is of vital importance.
Whether he becomes a blacksmith or a farmer,
he will discover not only its everyday use, but its
value in buying his food and clothing and the
furnishings for his house. In selling his wool or
buying sheep, the woolgrower will find his profits

largely in his skill in detecting the value of both
by feeling. The sense of touch discovers many defects which escape the best of eyes. If he becomes
a weaver, a watchmaker, a dealer in fine fabrics, a
surgeon, an oculist, a dentist, a musician, an
artist, a bank cashier, the possession of delicate
and finely discriminating touch is absolutely essential. It must ever be remembered that childhood is the only time when the resources of this
sense can be profitably developed. Fair efficiency
may be secured by beginning later in life, but rare
power is seldom attained. Some children inherit
great delicacy of touch, but whatever Nature sup-
plies them may be multiplied many fold by intelligent cultivation.

The extent to which touch is cultivated in
some of the schools for defectives is shown in the
skill with which the blind and deaf read raised
letters in English and German. Superintendent
Hammond states that Helen Kellar gets the
thought of a friend by placing her fingers on his
lips and her thumb on his throat as he speaks!
At the World's Fair she visited the art gallery,
and after passing her hand over the head and face
of several pieces of statuary, said of one, "*This
face feels sad.*" It was the statue of Melancholy!
She seems to have " brain cells in her finger tips."

CHAPTER VI.

THE SENSES (CONTINUED).—HEARING.

"Sweet is every sound,
The moan of doves in immemorial elms,
The murmuring of innumerable bees."

THE sense of hearing is the next in the order of Nature's wise and beneficent provisions for the child. All the senses thus far described are contact senses, but this one gives us information about objects far and near. Without it all existence would be as still as the chamber of death. Man's knowledge and man's pleasure would be curtailed beyond measure, while his progress in self-development would be exceedingly slow and difficult. The embarrassment which deafness in one ear produces is sad enough, but when both are bereft of the power to hear, much of life has gone out.

Authorities differ as to the stage of development of the ear at the time of the birth of the child, though the explanation is probably found in the fact that it varies in different children. In some, sounds are apparently appreciated almost immediately, while in others several hours or even days elapse before any kind of sound affects the child. A friend tells me that on the

31

morning after her babe was born it was frightened almost into convulsions by the explosion of a cannon firecracker near her window. Preyer says that his little son was surely deaf until the fourth day. Compayré reminds us that auditory sensibility wisely develops slowly: "By hearing too soon the child would run the risk of not hearing for the rest of his life. Too strong a vibration breaks the string of a harp or of a violin; so sounds too intense, if felt, would bruise or injure an organ so delicate and unexercised. Nature, then, has judiciously protected the child against the shock of too numerous or too violent sensations in leaving him dull of hearing for a few weeks." All this being true, it again emphasizes the necessity for intelligent, loving care during the very first weeks of the child's life. An old-time philosopher woke his children up every morning with sweet strains from his violin, lest a too violent shock might jar and disturb the harmony of the transition from sleep to wakefulness. What hushed and soothing *adagios* ought to awaken this babe and introduce him into the wonderful life he now enters!

If you are familiar with the internal structure of the ear, all of the above is easily understood. You can readily see that the delicate tympanic membrane at the base of the external auditory canal could not only be easily injured or broken by any sharp or loud noise, but by almost any kind of quick concussion which would force the air into the ear. It does not take much of a jar to disarrange the finely balanced machinery of the

middle or of the internal ear, and no care should
be considered too great for its protection. Children's diseases are just as likely to settle in a weak
spot as the diseases of adults, and for this reason
any slight disorder in the ear may soon become
serious. From various causes, these just mentioned being among them, authorities estimate
that from fifty to sixty per cent of the children
are more or less defective in hearing. It is also
claimed that by judicious treatment the percentage
can be reduced to fifteen or twenty. The advantage of a better acquaintance with this important
sense organ is thus further emphasized.

The diseases in and about children's ears often
become chronic very early in life and in many
families are a source of constant concern. Ordinary earache easily runs off into stabbing, stick-
ing pains, producing delirium, and leaving sore-
ness and tenderness in the whole side of the head
for days after. It is hardly possible to conceive a
more excruciating pain than that which frequently
accompanies discharges from the ear in scrofulous
children or in children who are recovering from
scarlatina, measles, smallpox, etc. Some children
seldom take a cold without inflammation of the
ear at once following. Often the trouble is in the
swelling and partial closing of the Eustachian tube,
or in the lodgment of an insect or of some hard
substance, or the accumulation of wax in the outer
canal, or in some affection of the mastoid bone
just above and behind the ear. But whatever or
wherever it is, it demands skillful and sympathetic
treatment. Usually danger gives notification in
6

slight deafness, in tingling sensations, in whistling
noises, and in characteristic buzzing and roaring
sounds hours or even days before severe pains force
attention. That which seems trifling at first may
become chronic and ineradicable in a fortnight,
hence the need for early attention to such symptoms. Every mother and every teacher ought to
be acquainted with simple remedies to apply, but
when these fail an aurist or a physician should be
consulted without delay.

In intellectual value the sense of hearing ranks
next to that of sight, though touch might possibly
with reason contend for the second place. It gives
us the three great characteristics of sound—pitch,
intensity, and quality or *timbre*—and also direction and distance by association and symbolism.
Distance is approximately determined by the intensity or volume of the sound as compared with
what we happen to know of it when near by, combined with changes in timbre, which experience
has taught us distance makes. So expert do travel-
ers and hunters become in estimating distance by
sound that it serves them almost as well as the eye.
The temperature and humidity of the air, together with its degree of homogeneousness, affect
all such estimates. Direction is discovered by the
relative intensity of the sound upon the two ears,
the short distance between them, combined with
the difference produced by their different relations to the line of the advancing sound waves,
being sufficient to enable very young children to
discriminate without much difficulty. If inability
to do this with reasonable certainty is discovered

in children of school age, it is sufficient cause for
further inquiry.

All normal ears easily recognize pitch in a
general way, though ability to distinguish clearly
the various tones of the diatonic scale comes with
education. Every child that can not readily distinguish high from low tones is defective, and if
reasonable effort fails to develop this power, it is
evidence of some organic defect that needs professional treatment. The proper test is simply to
produce sounds, first of marked difference in
pitch, as 1, 5, 8 of the scale; then of less difference,
as 1, 3, 5, 8; then the whole scale; then minor
divisions—sharps and flats. The voice or any
musical instrument may be used. It will sometimes be found that a child can distinguish pitch
in a piano or an organ, and not do it in vocal
tones, or in the latter and not in the former; and
yet, after a little practice, the inability may disappear. Where the physical ability is small, the
intellectual may come in to re-enforce it, and perception thus be easily exercised. On the other
hand, the former may be great and the latter so
weak that fine discrimination is impossible. Every
test made should keep these two elements constantly in mind. Much time is wasted in music
and reading in attempts to force pupils to recognize pitch without having given them any proper
training for developing ability to do it. There is
just the same necessity for a well-graded series of
exercises through a course of years for the cultivation of the physical side of pitch perception as for
the education of the muscles in writing or draw-

ing. It might as well be understood, once for all,
that skill in perception is attained only by intelligent exercise of the sense organs, and that every
attempt to get along without it must result in utter
failure. The organization of apperceptive organs
on the mental side is impossible without corresponding organization in the sensory ganglia.
Differences in pitch can no more be recognized,
except through corresponding nerve power in the
auditory apparatus, than can the different tones
be produced without properly trained vocal cords.
The self can react to interpret sounds through the
sensation only, and its multiplicity of shades is the
result of education.

To read well, talk well, sing well, play on any
musical instrument, or to enjoy vocal expression
or instrumental music of any kind requires a nice
appreciation of the varying shades of pitch.
Childhood is the best time for its cultivation,
though its growth should be directed and not unduly hastened. The child has plenty of time.
The rarest powers, as well as the rarest fruit, prefer
to take their own time for ripening. The range
of pitch perception should be constantly extending, while the fine shades of distinction are being
attained.

Tones are also distinguished by their quality
or timbre. By quality is meant that characteristic which enables us to distinguish among tones of
the same pitch and intensity; to recognize their
source as of a bird or of an organ, or of the human
voice, and the particular emotions they express.
Quality is due to the nature and number of over-

tones accompanying the fundamental or pitch tone. If a violin string be loosely made, the tone, whatever the pitch, will be more or less diffuse and rough; if it be compactly formed, the tone will have corresponding compactness and smoothness; so of a bell, solid or porous. This accounts for the difference in the quality of the voice as the vocal cords are inflamed or in the natural condition. Ears that hear at all usually appreciate emphatic differences in quality. The test is easily made by discovering whether a child can distinguish among voices of different persons, different forms of the same voice, vocal utterances of different animals, or the tones of different musical instruments, noises, etc. Surprising results will often show themselves in these tests. Where inability to make the general discriminations exists, the causes may be any of those already stated, and similar treatment should be used. Where children are to be handled in classes, those more ready in noting quality can afford to wait a little until the others approximate them in skill, though this suggestion should not be followed too rigidly.

Intensity, or volume, is the force or momentum of a sound and is dependent upon the swing or amplitude of the waves producing it. Ears that readily appreciate the other characteristics mentioned may still be unable to distinguish this one, at least with any degree of fineness. "*ff*" and "*pp*" mean about the same to them. Use same pitch, or same quality, with similar means, as suggested in preceding paragraphs, increasing and decreasing intensity, to discover effect upon the child. For, of course, effect on the child is the measure of the child's ability. Often sounds of great volume will produce intense pain. A child of mine could not be persuaded to stay near a brass band while it was playing because it gave her a severe earache. The ringing of a church bell drove a neighbor's child almost into convulsions. The curfew whistle is blowing as I write, and my dog falls prostrate as usual and begins a pitiful whine. All these and scores of other facts of a kindred nature will be discovered in testing hearing. It would be a feelingless and resourceless teacher or parent, indeed, who could not easily find ways of protecting and helping these sensitive children. A moment's thought would reverse the order now followed in many families.

The æsthetic value of the sense of hearing is too well known to need any elaboration. The art as well as the science of music is dependent entirely upon the ability of the ear to receive and transmit sounds of infinite variety in pitch and quality and intensity. As the rarest and noblest aspirations of the soul find expression in song, they are also awakened by song as it is received and interpreted by the refined sense of hearing. Among the fine arts, music is the first to minister to the child. The rhythm of the nurse's gentle lullaby quiets it almost the first hour after birth, and the sweet melodies of its early years soothe a thousand sorrows and transport it from many a turbulent passion to peaceful sleep—

Where dreams are songs,
And trundle-beds are fairies' chariots.

As music serves to express the emotions of youth and manhood, it rises in dignity and stateliness, finding its highest mission in voicing the longings of the human soul for the Infinite. By virtue of this intimate relationship to the finer sentiments, its ethical value can hardly be overestimated. A man with a cultivated ear has poor excuse for being immoral.

The value of this sense in a practical way is easily enough seen, but teachers and parents are often slow in understanding what its loss means to a child who is suffering from some affection which may injure or destroy it permanently. This chapter has already urged immediate attention to such cases, and they are mentioned again, with the hope that some poor child may be profited thereby.

Two seemingly parallel straight lines may be but an inch apart at their origin and yet be ten feet apart at the end of a mile. Some children are thirty years in growing deaf, some twenty, some ten, some five, some one!

There are too many partially deaf people in every community. Every such one is badly handicapped in his business and social relations. How many men lose good positions because of defective hearing! How many sad and fatal accidents are due to the same cause! The new education can do no better service to the oncoming generations than to preserve and perfect this sense in the children.

The clear understanding of language is dependent upon ability to hear well. Often the deepest meaning and the finest shades of thought

are lost because an accent, a subvocal, or a little
slur of the voice escapes notice. A child is thought
dull or stupid who could not be otherwise, for he
seldom hears anything that is said at home or in
the schoolroom. I visited a classroom not long
since, and found that pupils in the rear were cran-
ing their necks to see the diagrams on the board
and hear the explanations given. Some soon gave
up in despair and settled down in a listless way to
await the end of the recitation. Inquiry developed
the fact that nearly one third of them heard little
of any recitation. Under such conditions what
could be expected of them? A superintendent in
a small city reports that he found forty pupils in
his schools who were occupying rear forms and
who could hear little said by teacher or pupils at
the front.

Various general tests have been suggested, the
watch test being frequently named, but the human
voice is the best for the home and the classroom.
It is that which it is important the children should
hear. Let it be of the usual tone, and let children who hear it with difficulty be given seats near
the teacher, the others ranging back in the order
of ability to hear. Sight and the sense of temperature must also control in the assignment of seats,
as suggested in discussing them. In the home,
the place at the fireside and at the table, where
most of the talk can easily be heard, should always
be given to the child whose hearing is less acute
than that of the others. If proper care is observed,
such cases rapidly improve with opportunity and
exercise, and the defect usually entirely disappears.

CHAPTER VII.

THE SENSES (CONTINUED).—SIGHT.

WE are now to study the king of all the senses
—the sense of sight. It, like sound, is not a contact sense. Rays of light are transmitted through
space by an intangible medium called ether. So
faithfully does it do its duty that the eye is thus
permitted to see objects lying hundreds of millions
of miles away, a distance so great that no one can
form any adequate conception of it. While the
telephone transmits the human voice so that it can
be heard a thousand miles away, the telescope extends the power of the eye so that a vast multitude
of heavenly bodies are brought to view which
otherwise would not have been known to exist.
The wonderful resources of this sense and its vital
importance in every moment of our waking hours
give it the high place above assigned.

In structure its mechanism is not so difficult to
understand as that of the ear, though the rods
and cones underneath the retina perplex the student somewhat. At birth the eyes of some children are more fully developed than those of others, though it is probable that none of them at first
have more than the faintest sensation of light.
In a few days they begin to notice any bright light,

41

as that of a lamp, but the most painstaking investigators incline to the belief that there is very little
discrimination among objects for a fortnight, and
then only among those of bright colors.

Compayré reminds us that the child at first
sees only in front of him and that he does not see
objects to the right or left. This can be shown
easily by shifting a light or a bright colored object either way in front of him. He soon loses it
and gazes vacantly into space. The same authority
also cites the fact that all young children are myopic, seeing objects only at short range. The first
is due to the fact that the child has not yet learned
the art of moving its eyes so as to change the
field of vision; the second, to the fact that the eye
is not yet completely developed and that the power
of focal adjustment has not yet been attained.
Experiments of this nature during the first four
or five months of a child's life will reveal some
very interesting things about the growth of sight
perception, among them the surprising fact that
nearly all children are cross-eyed at birth and some
of them for many months after. The co-ordina-
tion of the movements of the muscles controlling
the eyeballs is necessary before rapid progress can
be made in distinguishing objects by sight; this is
often not fully attained before the age of four or
five.

The intellectual value of this sense needs no
particular discussion here. So much of our knowledge comes through it that the value of the other
senses is often overlooked. If one sees a thing,
he is supposed to know all about it. Seeing has

become the synonym for understanding, and when we have explained a matter to any one we quickly ask, " Do you see it? " The direct knowledge given us by the eye is of hue, tint, and intensity. By hue is meant the more or less positively defined colors; by tint, the varying shades due simply to the small quantity of a color or hue showing itself in a mixture or background of white or some leading color; by intensity, the amount of light received from an object by the eye. The first is dependent upon the relative rapidity of the wave movements, red being the lowest and violet the highest; the second and third are already sufficiently explained. By the infinite number of combinations of these three, the perception of the external world is made so definite that no two human beings out of the billion and a half now living appear exactly alike to the cultivated eye; no two of the endless quintillions of leaves that cover the earth are found to agree in every detail. Everywhere is variety; the bright and the somber, the red and the gold, the light and the dark, the green and the yellow, the blue and the crimson, the glow of the evening sunset, the dancing of the silver-tipped waves, the wild sprangles of the restless lightning, are ever revealing through the eye the nature and the resources of the universe of matter and of force.

The purely visual function of the eye is greatly multiplied and extended by its union with the muscular movements of the body, the neck, and the eyeballs, as already intimated. By the aid of the first two the whole range of the horizon, around and above, can be swept almost in an instant, and objects distinguished and located with surprising accuracy. At first consciously, then more or less unconsciously, the muscular sensations serve as a measure of the angles passed over in the movement and the visual sensation is the only one prominent in the perception. But when the eyeballs of children of school age or of adults are observed, they will be seen to be as restless as globules of mercury, turning hither and thither and everywhere on the slightest occasion. Few of these movements are purposeless. They are made so as to take in the whole of an object and its surroundings; they are repeated and reversed again and again, that each detail of color and tint and shade and form and relation may be verified. These muscular sensations also merge in consciousness with the purely visual, and the knowledge derived is usually attributed to the latter. Then there are two sets of delicate ciliary muscles inside the eyeball itself; one adjusts the size of the pupil so that the proper amount of light may be admitted to the internal eye, the other adjusts the lenses of the eye in looking at objects at varying distances, so as to focus the rays coming from them upon the retina. Though the movements of these internal muscles are so slight, they evidently enter into conscious sensation fully enough to assist eye-perception in determining the shape, distance, and size of objects.

The dependence of sight upon touch has already been mentioned. At first all objects seem flat to the child, and right up against him, as it were. Exercising a natural impulse to touch them, he puts out his hand and finds that they are a little distance from him, or even beyond his reach. Through a long course of experimenting, he learns to measure in a rough way the distance to any object by the amount of muscular effort necessary to reach it. In like manner also he gets an idea. of its form and size, including its depth as well as its height and breadth. The eye follows all these movements, and the associated visual and muscular sensations of the eye proper become so assimilated with them that on their recurrence, without touch, they serve to symbolize the touch sensations, and thus give knowledge which touch alone had been supplying. So by this wonderful principle of symbolism the eye gradually usurps this function of touch, and tells us whether objects are rough or smooth, liquid or solid, fibrous or crystalline, round or elliptical, oblong or square, flat or in relief, sharp or dull, large or small, fixed or moving, far or near; and all of this by the minute differences seen in the shades and colors of the various parts of a body or of different bodies. Thus it not only enhances the value of touch, but makes itself almost a universal sense, for this principle of symbolism enables it to act in place of other senses also, as explained in Chapter II.

The æsthetic value of the senses also reaches its climax in the sense of sight. Bright colors awaken interest and pleasure in a very young child. Their combinations in almost any fantastic way gratify and delight him. With the development of his intellectual nature the feeling of harmony is aroused only as certain colors are associated, and, later, æsthetic taste finds satisfaction in tints and colors of the rarer hue.

Even in the most cultivated minds Nature and art never cease to kindle the emotion of beauty through color and shade alone. But the perception of form, as touch drops out, also awakens the emotion of the beautiful. Order, proportion, symmetry, and grace in form appeal to the finer and less sensuous elements of our nature more easily than does color. Form itself serves to purify and spiritualize the æsthetic feelings. Certain classes of movements, particularly those of animals, possibly due to the concrete forms they suggest, beget similar emotions. When color and form and movement are harmoniously combined, the most pleasurable effects are produced.

A liberal education and a successful life are so clearly dependent upon the perfection and skill in the use of the eyes that their care and training ought to constitute a large part of the responsibility of every parent and teacher. It is a long distance from that vacant, expressionless look of the newborn babe to that eye so full of meaning and understanding in the richly endowed man, and some intelligent hand must help to its attainment. The aid to give children with normal eyes is suggested in the next chapter.

In certain families almost every child is troubled with some affection of the eye; in others, weak or diseased eyes are unknown. Heredity shows its trail in no other sense more clearly. Many of these diseases are of the eyelids, not affecting the eyeball at all, and are merely temporary; others, though external, are very serious and gradually extend to the eyeball, even to the optic nerve. The surface of the eyeball is subject to diseases of a similar nature, sometimes originating there and extending to the eyelids. All such disorders should be treated by physicians or by experienced nurses. The orders they give should be strictly followed, even though "there is no danger." Many eyes have been ruined by the carelessness or indifference of those whose love and interest ought to have taught them better.

These disorders are easily seen, but those that directly affect the sense of sight are usually discoverable only by closer examination. The experiments with the lighted candle or lamp for discovering the first sight sensations, range of field to right and left, distance at which objects are evidently lost to view, constitute a series which should be repeated at first from day to day, and then from week to week until such time as there seems to be but little change. The progress, rapid or slow, which the child makes in extending his range of vision by association with muscular movements and with touch should be most carefully noted. At times he will be found to have made great progress, and too much care can not be taken to discover the cause. Bright objects, as balls of colored yarn, may early be substituted for the lighted candle, afterward being varied with those of softer colors. *No attempt should be made to stimulate the eye to undue activity nor to test its endurance at any time, particularly with little chil-*

dren. The eyes of children are often injured greatly by gazing too long at a bright light. I remember, when past thirty, experimenting with an electric light to discover its power, and, though I was soon able to stare it out of countenance, I found, as the cars started off, that I was totally blind. Fortunately, the paralysis was temporary, but how much the contest has affected my sight since has always been a problem. A student of mine was blind for several days and suffered with weak eyes for years as a result of walking a mile at midday with the reflections of the bright sunlight from the snow crystals pouring into her face at every step. Reading from a brightly illuminated page has a similar effect. These experiences are so common and so well known that any one who endangers a child's eyes in such a way is little short of a criminal.

Should these experiments with the babe reveal any peculiarity at any time, there ought to be no alarm. It sometimes happens that a child appears to be making considerable progress for several days and then apparently loses all power gained. The cause may be interest in something else, or weariness, or a slight temporary weakness in the eyes. If the child is later in observing the light than other children, it may be the better for him, as earlier appreciation might do him harm. If, however, he pays no attention to it when ten days old, a physician's advice should be promptly sought, possibly even before that time if suspicions are aroused. Should the retrogression above mentioned continue for a few days, or should no progress be making, the same ever-safe counselor should be called in.

Not only should objects of different colors be used, but also of different sizes and forms, especially as the child is running around and getting acquainted with the outside world. Though, as stated, all small children are short-sighted to some extent, ability to adjust the eye to objects within reasonable range should be clearly showing itself as the child enters school. If parents do their duty, they will inform the teacher of any defects in vision. By noting the ease or difficulty with which the children read writing on the blackboard or the words in their books, teachers will at once discover reasons for further tests. The short-sighted children should be placed where they can see the work on the board, and they should be permitted to keep their eyes near the paper as they read or copy or figure. Weak eyes should not be confused with myopic eyes, for the former see with difficulty at any distance, while the latter see easily within their own range. The former need more light; the latter, a proper focus, which proper distance only can give, though suitable glasses will aid both. Among older children, long-sighted, hyperopic, eyes will occasionally be discovered. In serious cases of myopia or hyperopia, expert oculists should be consulted and proper glasses secured. The reason for consulting a specialist is that the child should not only have glasses that will enable him to see well, but that will also serve to gradually correct his defect. Where the cases are not very serious, the child

should be seated in the schoolroom as suggested,
and permitted to hold his book or paper at the
distance best adapted to his eyes. He should,
however, be encouraged in a friendly way to move
his book a little nearer the normal distance from
time to time, in order to stimulate readjustment
to the new focus. There should be no haste about
this, for if the child has made appreciable progress in correcting defects in four or five years it
is cause for congratulation. It is probable that
the increase in skill in apprehending words and
objects will also relieve the embarrassment in myopic and hyperopic children, as they soon learn
to get along without such clear eye pictures as
their more fortunate neighbors are accustomed to
have.

The most difficult cases to manage are those
known as astigmatic, and those in which the foci
of the two eyes are at unequal distances, thus con-
fusing the image, particularly at certain ranges.
There seems to be no remedy for these defects save
in glasses properly fitted. The former is quite common, and is a prolific source of headache. Thousands of cases of chronic headache have been
promptly cured by the use of glasses. Though the
astigmatism may be very slight, the constant strain
on the fine nerves and muscles of the internal eye
produces most acute pain in the head. This same
effort in myopic and hyperopic cases produces the
same result. A ministerial friend tells me that a
teacher forced his son, who was afflicted with myopia, to hold his book at the "regulation distance" and in the regulation position as he read

or studied, and that the headache resulting threw him into such nervous disorders that at least once a fortnight he was obliged to keep him out of school for three or four days. A lady friend tells me that her little daughter had been coming home every day for months with a bad headache, and that she was losing all interest in school, when the writer visited the city and urged the teachers to test the sight and hearing of their pupils. This girl was found defective in eyesight and given a front seat. In two weeks her headache was all gone, and her interest in school had returned. A multitude of similar cases might be given, but these must suffice. If this paragraph awakens its readers to a fuller understanding of the intimate connection between overstrained eyes and headache among children and adults, somebody will be remembered most kindly by them.

For a little more definite test of the defects just named, Snellin's cards, bought of jewelers and dealers in spectacles nearly everywhere for ten cents, will be found serviceable.

The fact has already been mentioned that the eyes of little children are often crossed more or less, and that the power to move both together may develop but slowly. It is important that nothing be done which will tend to cause a child to try to look in two directions at the same time. Slowly moving an object not too small, in various directions at some distance before him, carefully excluding anything from the right or left which might attract him, will encourage the two eyes to move together. This repeated from day to day will assist the child in co-ordinating the muscles and attaining the power to move them together. Very small objects should not be used, neither should anything be placed so near as to force the child to try to look over his nose. The disposition to show a child off by having him look cross-eyed is vicious and criminal.

Cataract is a well-known disease of the eye, but its early symptoms often escape notice, and sight is gone before any attempt is made to preserve it. At the first suggestion of a discoloration of the pupil, medical aid should be sought.

Children are continually getting something in their eyes—a particle of dust, a cinder, a thorn—and everybody ought to know how to remove it. Put a toothpick above the eyelid and quickly reverse the lid over it, thus usually exposing the foreign substance. With a silk handkerchief gently remove the intruder. If the substance be imbedded in the eyeball, great care must be exercised lest permanent injury result to it. Only an expert should be permitted to handle this delicate organ if the case be serious.

In the selection of text-books and reading matter generally for children, fine print and masses of letters and figures should be avoided. Eyes may be ruined in a fortnight by too close application to solid matter of this kind. In visiting a class recently, I found twenty boys, fourteen to seventeen years of age, complaining about weak eyes. Many of them had never thought of weak eyes before entering the class, but a month of study over fine print and compact columns had caused them incalculable distress. Good, clear type, well leaded, on white paper will prevent such trouble. Some blackboards are not fit for use. Half of the pupils do not write their work on the board so that it can be seen without strain. The light in many schoolrooms is very poor; often too much, often not enough; often from the right when it ought to be from the left.

CHAPTER VIII.

THE SENSES (CONTINUED).—GENERAL FUNCTIONS.

WE have now become somewhat acquainted with each of the senses, its specific nature, its particular office or function, its value in an intellectual, æsthetic, and practical way, the diseases to which it is subject, the tests which may be applied in discovering defects, and some of the methods to be used in correcting them; we have also discovered the importance of all this information in the education of the child. It remains for us to inquire into the general functions of the senses, and to find their further relation to his physical and mental life.

Whatever may be our theories regarding the exact nature of the mental power with which the child is endowed at birth, all agree that without some means of receiving communication from the material world outside the mind must lie dormant, no development resulting. The senses furnish this means of communication. Though we are ignorant of the nature of the connection between the nerve cells of the brain and the mind, of the way in which certain kinds of nerve excitation are unerringly given practically the same meaning by one and all minds, we are not without some definite knowledge of the way in which these external objects awaken brain activity. Each nerve filament has direct communication with the brain, so that we may regard the nervous organism as a great telegraphic or telephonic system, with the brain as the receiving or central station. If a nerve filament capable of appreciating heat motion is excited by a warm body in contact, by concussion, by friction, or by chemical action, the excitation is carried on its own nerve line to the brain, and there entering consciousness is interpreted as heat. In no other way can a child get knowledge of temperature. If a terminal filament capable of appreciating pressure be excited by some body coming against it, that peculiar kind of nerve excitement is also carried to the brain by its connecting line. In that way only can a child get knowledge of the presence of an external body and of the nature of its surface. In a similar way stimuli act, each in its own way, upon the various sensory nerve filaments, producing specific kinds of nerve excitation, thus making the child acquainted with the characteristics of the world of external objects. The fidelity with which this transmission is made determines, in great part, the extent and accuracy of the child's knowledge. If this delicate machinery is not in perfect order, not working with precision, confusion naturally results.

As you are observing the children, you will see how rapidly they grow in power to distinguish objects and to note their qualities. The more frequently a sense is excited within certain bounds, and with slightly varying stimuli, the more sensitive it becomes and the finer the distinctions it presents to the mind. The physical senses as the media of communication between the mind and the external world serve their full purpose only as they are gaining in ability to appropriate and transmit an increasing number of shades of differences in color, in tone, in form, in intensity. The mind can proceed no faster in gaining power to make such discrimination than the senses, hence the need for the intelligent selection of means and methods that their progress may be as rapid and as economical as possible; hence also the reminder that every educational scheme which is not based upon sense-perception must fail.

At that point where the self and the not-self meet, the mind must respond, or nothing but brain activity results. The clock may strike a thousand times, objects may pass many times back and forth before the eyes, the fragrance of flowers fill every corner of the room, but unless the mind gives special attention no sensations proper are aroused, and one sits oblivious to it all. These excitations do enter in a slight way into consciousness, however, making up a sort of substratum—a *sensation continuum*, as Dr. Dewey and others call it—which affects more or less the general tone of the self, no matter in what it happens to be absorbed at the time. Any one of them may be quickly exalted into consciousness and made the special object of attention, while the others are left still involved in the subconscious mass. This may be illustrated at any time by suddenly stopping whatever you may be doing and noting, one after another, the many things which you were really seeing and hearing and feeling and even tasting and smelling, and yet of which you were not at all conscious. This experiment will enable you to see clearly that unless the mind specifically differentiates a sensation from its companions and interprets it, gives it meaning, and associates it with the object producing it, there can be no knowledge gained. The sensation itself is not knowledge, but without it there could be no knowledge. It is pure feeling, and becomes knowledge only as it is given meaning. Active as a physical force speeding its way to the brain, it can do nothing now but passively wait at the portal for the mind to take hold of it and give it meaning. Its various characteristics, due to its sources, soon become familiar to the mind, and sensation and object seem merged in one.

Sensations occupy a more prominent part in the life of the child than of the adult, for they are practically his only mental food. What a man would discover about an object by reflection and reason, the child finds out only through the senses. He must pull it, bite it, stamp on it, look down its mouth, smell it, scratch it, throw it about, no matter whether it be a kitten or a brownie. He tears the choicest rose to pieces, because that is the only way he can find out what is inside. He pounds away on a drum or an old tin pan, because it affords him pleasing entertainment, and in that way he learns something about it. His mind feeds

on sensations just as the body feeds on bread and
meat. He is naturally as hungry for them as he
is for his meals. To deny them to him is to do
him as much harm as to deny him food. As we
take pains in supplying the latter, the former
should with equal intelligence and with equal lib-
erality be provided for him. By this it should not
be understood that he is to be permitted to destroy everything that he can get his hands on—
though there ought to be many things given him
for that purpose if he so inclines—but that objects
in variety, particularly from the outside world,
should always be at his disposal, always be coming
into his little world. Many children would do less
damage to the furniture if this propensity could
only be given indulgence by allowing them to tear
some worthless things to bits once in a while. It
needs direction, not suppression—direction not in
a specific way in these early years, but in a general
way. There are thousands of things with which
he may become familiar by such management, and
that too without realizing that he is making any
special effort to learn. This informal education in
these years is just as important as the formal education of the schoolroom which he is soon to enter.

The sensations thus constantly crowding in
upon the child will, however, give him little valuable knowledge unless he be wisely, though in-
formally, guided in getting the meaning out of
them. He must be helped to understand them.
With very little aid he will make great progress
himself. Each discovery of a new power or activity in himself will give him entertainment for a

whole day. He may make mistakes without number, but care will sooner or later bring him around to correct most of them himself. There is no need for worry that he is losing a multitude of opportunities to learn things. A thousand acorns are destroyed where one grows into a tree, and ten thousand flowers bloom where one produces fruit. The wise child is that one who knows everything he sees; not the one who can tell all the stories he has had read to him.

Furnishing, then, as the senses do, the materials which are to be worked up into knowledge, everything said in the preceding chapters concerning their relation to the mind and concerning the importance of keeping them in vigorous, healthy condition ought to be growing more clear. It is important that weakness or latency or disease in any sense organ receive special attention as already suggested, but in our zeal we must not forget that the normal children may be going wrong through our neglect. In her efforts to encourage a delicate appetite in one child, a mother may allow another to become the slave of an artificial or uncontrolled appetite. In shielding one from excessive use of his eyes, she may overlook the fact that another is losing his eyesight in reading fine print or in trying to write fine copies for his teacher in penmanship. If boys and girls with perfect senses are making no greater progress in sense-perception than their less fortunate mates, somebody is at fault. They ought to be advancing more rapidly in making nice distinctions and accurate observations than their defective classmates.

CHAPTER IX.

CONSCIOUSNESS AND APPERCEPTION.

THE bridge over from the physical to the mental is found in consciousness. For our present purpose consciousness may be defined as the self knowing its own states or activities. It is that which distinguishes the animal from the plant, and which in the child enables him to recognize himself as a thinking, feeling, self-active being. It enters into every mental activity, and is the one great characteristic of all minds. For this reason many authorities prefer to call the various mental activities phases of consciousness.

As heretofore explained, external forces, no matter how tumultuously they may assail the nervous organism, nor how faithfully they may be carried to the brain, can not enter the mind save through the door of consciousness. Even pain, as a toothache or a headache, slips below consciousness when something else is given a place in it. The power to adjust the mind so as to give one sensation a place in consciousness to the exclusion of others is just as much a matter of attainment as any other power mentioned in this book. Harriet Martineau as a young girl visited the seashore with some friends, and, being of a very

nervous disposition, was so excited that she at first
was unable to see the breakers or to hear them
beating against the rocks. Observe the children
in your circle for a few days, and note how often
they have similar experiences.

Note also how quickly a child becomes interested and so wholly absorbed in some object that
it is difficult to turn his attention to anything
else. Probably in some cases it is pure willfulness, but it is more often due to our inability to
get into his consciousness. He does not hear, because he is seeing. He does not see, because he
is hearing. He does not hear nor see you, because he is seeing or hearing something else. He
may not have more pleasure in it than he would
in you or in what you are trying to offer him, but
the latter simply does not get into his consciousness sufficiently, if at all. I have two very little
friends who, I am assured, love me and frequently
call up good times they have had with me, but I
often pass them with a friendly " Good morning " that does not affect them any more than it
does the man in the moon. This explains why
children often do not hear when mother calls.
Illustrative of the opposite, however, is the case
of a little friend that quietly notified her mother,
who had spent some minutes calling her, though
she was lying in the grass near by, that she was
" playing cow, and so, of course, couldn't hear! "

By its function consciousness is a differentiating activity, and, as the sensory ganglia in the
brain of the newborn babe are scarcely differentiated, there is little or nothing to come into con-

sciousness with any degree of distinctness. Discomfort or pain, without location or definition, causes him to cry, but the effort is purely reflexive. It is possible that by his very cry he rouses consciousness to recognize sound as distinct from pain if perchance the latter has in some manner already found a place there. Consciousness knows feelings, states, as well as activities, and the continuation or repetition of any new and marked sensation is Nature's method of starting the mental life of the child. How feeble must be this first glimmer in conscious life! But it is a glimmer, and it is of life! The movement thus begun enables consciousness to distinguish the different senses from each other, and then the different affections of the same sense, as already explained, expanding and strengthening at every step.

In these early days the child lies enveloped in a mass of common feeling, almost exclusively sensuous, and the pleasure that comes as one feeling after another is slightly lifted above its companion feelings in consciousness is just as grateful to him as the satisfaction which food brings to his appetite.

But while consciousness is discovering differences in these feelings, in some way also one feeling begins to remind the child of another which he once experienced, and the two great relations which enter into all knowledge, *difference and identity,* are recognized. What are these relations? Simply of difference and likeness in certain sensations or feelings. But the grasping of these relations constitutes knowledge. As a new sensation

comes into consciousness, the only meaning which
it can get is that it is like another which was once
there. Slowly, yet rapidly enough for the safety
of the brain, skill in recognizing this likeness and
its opposite, unlikeness, comes to the child. Many
times the new is interpreted by means of the old
until the mind becomes less dependent upon the
latter, and gets the meaning of the new immediately by " reading itself into it." This process is
called *apperception*. As consciousness begins .as-
serting itself, each succeeding effort reacts upon
it, as exercise reacts upon a hand or arm, increasing its strength and skill, and gives it added power
to act in similar lines. So to the interpretation or
to the discovery of relation in each new sensation
it brings increased ability. This reaction, this
effect upon the self after each effort, is called *retention*. Understanding this, you can see that
whereas in the first acquaintance with a new sensation or experience we consciously bring the old
to bear upon it to find out its likeness or difference, we are afterward able to bring the self, as
organized by the past experiences, to bear upon it,
and thus get its meaning at once without conscious comparison. This is what is meant by
" reading one's self into it." You can also easily
see that, in whatever general lines a child may be
exercising his activity, his apperceptive powers,
or so-called apperceptive organs, will be cor-
respondingly increased. If he uses his eyes, he
will soon attain skill in interpreting eye sensations; if his ears, in interpreting sound. If he
live among miners, he will the more readily dis-

cern anything pertaining to mining; if among
sailors, anything pertaining to the sea; if among
farmers, anything pertaining to the farm. As he
exercises his mind in counting, he becomes skilled
in the art of computation; in classifying plants, he
gains in ability to distinguish flowers and fruits;
in naming the stars, he rises to a ready apprehension of the constellations. It is for this reason
that the same experience means one thing to a
scientist and another thing to a merchant; that a
piece of marble means one thing to a sculptor and
another to a geologist; that a jardinière of delicately branching plants means a vase of maiden-
hair ferns to one child and " a pot of green feath-
ers " to another: that the word reed means a long,
slender grass stalk to the son of a countryman and
a thin strip of brass to the son of an organ-maker;
that the cross is a symbol of freedom to one man
and of oppression to another.

Everything that comes into the life of the
child, whether through his environment, his occupation, his companions, or his books, affects
him, organizes him, in such a way as to determine
in great measure the meaning which he will put
into and get out of each succeeding experience.
However strange it may seem, *the only meaning a
child gets out of a thing is that which he puts into it.*
Whatever he is himself he will in kind be getting
out of each new experience. If you wish to find
out all about a boy, get him to express himself
freely in words and actions about some thing
which you can bring to his notice. His words
and actions are approximately about the object,

but they are as truly about himself. In them he reveals what he knows, what he is, as clearly as a burnished mirror reflects his ruddy face; indeed, the only thing he sees in an object is himself, and it is himself that he reads not *into* but *in* that object.

Put a robin's egg or nest on the desk and adroitly get the boys and girls to talking about it at recess while you are apparently busy at something else. Take mental notes and write them out afterward. Test them in the same way with a tadpole, a violet, a strawberry, a snail, a praying mantis, a butterfly, a dragon fly, a cotton plant, a lump of anthracite coal, and you will soon learn more about those children and their homes—what they talk about, what they read, where they have been, what they are thinking about, what kind of language they use, what manners they have, what ideas of right and wrong, what they lack, what they retain, whether they are accurate or loose in their observations, whether they reason well or poorly—than you could learn in a whole year by direct questions.

Give a child an idea of a rectangle, and start him around to find all the rectangles he can see in the room. He will name the windows, the doors, the blackboards, the slates, the desks, the books, the walls, the ceiling, the panes of glass. Try him again with a circle, a triangle, with an idea of wood, of cloth, of a nail head, a leaf, a pencil, a chair. In all cases he will recognize these in objects presented to him only as he is able to see that in them which is in himself as idea. This

8

simple principle, so easily verified in children, controls every onward movement in knowledge-getting, however slight, and a thorough understanding of it is essential to any profitable study of their development.

A few simple experiments additional will help us to formulate the laws in accordance with which apperception acts. Give a child a piece of candy. He instantly puts it into his mouth and gets pleasure out of it. Some time after, let him choose from several articles in your hand, among which is a stick of candy like the former, and he promptly picks it up. Vary the test from time to time with sticks of differing forms and colors. As long as the likeness is evident the recognition is ready enough. Gradually his knowledge extends until he will with fair certainty pick candy of any form or color from among a variety of articles, even though some of them may be round and colored so as at least to suggest the first stick he ate. It does not take any one long to see that similarity in form or color enables the child to discover the second as a stick of candy, and also to see that the association of the sweet taste with that of form and color in the one experience was sufficient to suggest sweet taste again when the form and color in the second stick were recognized. He could see by similarity that the second was a stick of candy, and that, being a stick of candy, it must also be sweet. In both cases he reads his former experience into it, and gets its meaning as a stick of candy. The law of apperception by similarity, then, may be stated as follows:

When the mind recognizes elements in an experience as similar to those in a previous experience, it immediately gives the new experience the same meaning as the old.

This law is dependent upon the great law of association which may now be stated:

The elements of which any experience is composed become so related in the mind by the association that the recurrence of one tends to bring back the others.

This law not only makes apperception but all knowledge-getting possible. At sight of the stick of candy, the sensation of taste also returns to the mind; at sight of a hot poker, the fact that it will burn comes back to the child; at sound of the bark of the dog, comes also the picture of the dog; at the touch of its fur, the picture of a cat and of its sharp claws; at sight of the chair, the picture of a man sitting on it; at the sound of the clock striking the hour of nine, the children singing the Gloria for the opening of school. These last illustrations show how contiguity in time or place may help the apperceptive process as well as similarity.

It must be clear enough to any teacher that the principle of apperception sufficiently explains the need for a sequence of studies and of subjects in each study, so that the learning process will be easy, natural, economical. It also shows that any method of instruction which adheres strictly to the class plan and ignores the differences in the individual pupils is illogical and wasteful. It is more important that the teacher find out the facts

already mentioned in this chapter concerning the
kind and extent of each child's knowledge, together with his skill in using what he knows in
getting further knowledge, than that he should
have all of the information which the best set of
school records in the world can give. The best
training which can be given a child is not that
which fills his head with facts, but that which
enables him to use to the best possible advantage
the facts which he does get. The man with small
capital and great capacity is sure to be rich; the
man with great capital and little capacity will soon
be poor. The principle holds just as well in the
mental and spiritual world.

CHAPTER X.

APPERCEPTION (CONTINUED).—ATTENTION.

THE reason that a certain experience means one thing to one child and another to a second is due in large measure, as has been explained, to the differences in their previous experiences and education. If a rabbit is brought into the room, one child will flee from it, while another will immediately fondle it; one will notice its color, another its fur, another its ears, another its tail, another its teeth, another its eyes, another the way it runs. If a doll is brought in, one will speak of its clothes, another of its face, another of its hands, another of its hair, another of the material of which it is made. If you pronounce the word corn to the children, one will think of canned corn, another of popcorn, another of corn growing in the field, another of corn meal, another of sweet corn, another of Kaffir corn, another of broom corn, another of the corn on father's big toe; still others may think of a grain of corn, its shape, its color, its size, its use, etc.

An additional reason for this great variety in the things first noticed and first mentioned by them will be found, if you carry the experiments far enough, in the fact that they are the ones in

which for the time at least the children are most
interested. This interest is caused by the pleasure which is given the child at the time or which
it has experienced in the past. The pleasure may
be enhanced by the familiarity or the novelty of
the object, or of some element or elements in it.
It may be sensuous or intellectual, real or imagined. It is this which gives it value. Anything has value for us which has power to contribute to our enjoyment. The fur of the rabbit
is soft to the touch, and so delights the child;
the snow-white of its tail in contrast with the
brownish gray of its body pleases the eye, and so
he becomes interested in its color. The bright
ribbons on the doll stimulate the optic nerve, and
interest is quickened at once. The mention of
corn calls up the roasting ears at yesterday's dinner, because of the enjoyment they furnished. It
must be remembered that the term pleasure is applied to every kind of feeling, whatever its source,
which is in harmony with our being. Its opposite term, pain, is applied to feelings not in harmony with it. Interest may arise from the latter
as well as from pleasure, and so value may be
either positive or negative. Value may be natural
or acquired—that is, it may belong to the object
itself or it may be due to the particular meaning
it has for us. Two knives may be exactly alike,
but one is a present from mother, and therefore
is worth a thousand times as much as the other.
A lock of hair may be soft and silken, and as such
please all who look at it, but to the one who recognizes it as the dear curls of a loved baby it has

value and interest which is beyond computation.
A lump of silver ore lying on the mountain side
is nothing but an ordinary stone to us, but it sets
the imagination of an experienced miner on fire.
The more knowledge one may have about an object the greater will be the variety of interest it
arouses.

The reason a child picks out one object from
among several is found, then, in the interest it
arouses in him, or in the value it has for him because of its ability to arouse pleasure. It is for
the same reason that he selects and exalts above
the others some particular element in an object,
as, for instance, its color, its shape, its texture, its
taste, its odor, its utility, its past associations. The
following laws may easily be verified:

*The mind attaches most value to that which
gives it most pleasure, antipicated or realized.*

*Whatever gives or promises pleasure or pain
to the child awakens interest.*

*The element in an experience which possesses
the most value to the child comes at once into
prominence in consciousness, the others taking a
subordinate place in apperception or dropping out
of notice entirely.*

The first may be called the law of value; the
second, the law of interest; the third, the law of
disengagement or of dissociation. If it were not
for these laws, everything would mean practically
the same thing to us, and differentiation would
be a very laborious and unsatisfactory process.
Without interest, knowledge would be shorn of
much of its charm and life of all its zest. It

breaks up monotony, and constantly incites the mind to new adjustments. These laws lie at the basis of educational principles, and no method of instruction can wisely ignore them.

As stated before, a variety of elements, of sensations, always lie in mass in consciousness. Some force is necessary to push or pull one of them into prominence. If one of the stimuli have sufficient value in the way of intensity or quality or pitch to arouse interest, pain or pleasure, consciousness immediately apprehends it, and it becomes the object of attention. This is the reason we increase the volume of the voice or change its quality in order to attract the attention of one who is absorbed in something else. A very small child soon learns the philosophy of such a course, and so cries louder or with a different tone in case mother does not promptly respond.

When the mind is concentrated upon some particular element in an experience, it is said to be giving attention. This is essential to all apperception, to all knowledge. The reason for the selection of a particular element to the exclusion of others has already been sufficiently explained. The isolation from the others must be so complete that it will not be confused with them. That being secured, the self must be brought to bear upon that element by adjusting all of its powers to it so as to find its meaning. There is very great difference in merely looking at a thing to the exclusion of other things, and in turning the whole of one's activities upon it in order to interpret it. There will be no meaning in it until the mind dis-

covers correspondence between the new elements
and those with which it is already familiar. It is
for this reason that rapidity in adjustment should
be sought constantly. Many children wear their
eyes out staring at a thing, imagining that they
are giving attention. If they are not at the same
time actively engaged in fitting themselves to it,
as it were, there is little hope of their becoming
any the wiser. A further word in the way of illustration may be in place. A child was given a key.
He immediately toddled to the door and tried to
insert it in the keyhole. Had he not brought to
bear upon it his past knowledge and discovered
identity or likeness, such a movement would have
had no significance whatever. I gave a word,
felicific, to a class of young men and women not
long since. It had no meaning to them, in spite
of all their efforts to " remember." I suggested a
division of the word, and lo! one of them saw at
once his old friends *felix* and *felicity*, and another
recognized in *fic* the essence of *fiction*, and they
were not Latin students either. A little practice
following enabled them to adjust their knowledge
of words to the interpretation of many strangers
with surprising facility. I stepped off the train
once at midnight in a blinding storm and started
to find a hotel I had been told was not far away.
I soon discovered that I was lost, when a flash of
lightning, though lasting but an instant, revealed
a score of objects to me. Almost before it was
gone I had brought to bear upon them all the
description given me, and had located the hotel so
accurately that I was able to go directly to its door.

Accuracy is as important in the adjustment as rapidity. In one sense, we may say that there is really no adjustment that is not accurate. If the process lack intelligence and self-control, flurry, confusion, and waste must result. There is a kind of superficial adjustment which comes so easily and so quickly that the deeper meanings are entirely overlooked. Dr. Baldwin very aptly calls such attention liquid attention, for it as quickly loses the effect of the new knowledge as water loses the form of the vessel from which it has been poured.

Follow up all of this with a variety of tests and experiments, and discover how and why children differ in the rapidity and accuracy of their adjustment to common things. Find how easily they are deceived and how quickly they learn to adjust themselves with greater ease.

Apperception is not complete, however, until this adjustment has resulted in uniting or identifying the new element with others already familiar to the mind. The disengagement which took it away from its companion elements in consciousness makes possible its association and alliance with others of its own kind and name. The recognition of some such relationship is, of course, essential to the adjustment already described, but the final stage reacts, intensifies, and reaffirms the identification and assimilation, so that the meaning takes definite form as an idea. The idea may be simple or complex, depending upon the number of elements which the mind may relate and combine with it. Practice enables the child to hold in mind an increasing number of relations, and his attention becomes " many-sided "—that is, he is able to apprehend and give meaning at once to many elements in an experience.

Hold some strange object before the class for an instant, then discover how many things each pupil can name in writing about it. Find out, if possible, why some of them saw so little in it. Their own explanations may be of value in adapting means and methods to their needs.

The term relation has been used several times, and its meaning ought not to be misunderstood. *It is simply the connection which the mind gives objects because of the discovery of common or like elements.* It is that which enables a child to connect or to see the whole in the part, the cause in the effect, the class in the individual, the resemblance or contrast of one object with another in color, or form, or size, or texture. It leads to all identification and differentiation. By it knowledge rises from the individual to the class, the relation, the common element, becoming more ideal and more universal with each succeeding experience.

CHAPTER XI.

SYMBOLISM.

EACH object in the universe is the expression of an idea. No flower of the field, no pebble by the wayside, no bird that skims the air, no star that glimmers in the wide expanse of heaven, can be what it is save as the realization, the concrete individual expression of that which first existed as idea. Each stands as the sign of the idea out of which it was born. That idea is its true meaning, and it is that, and that alone, which we strive to find in all knowledge-getting. A child wishes to communicate the idea to me that he has . hurt his finger; he holds it up and moans. In getting the meaning of his gesture and cry, I am simply getting the idea of which they are the expression or the sign. He brings an apple and a knife and lays them on my lap. The meaning of this act is the idea that originated and directed it. He utters a word, and its meaning is the idea he chose it to express. He draws a rough picture; it is meaningless save as I find the idea prompting it. What is true of everything that the child or the man creates or does is also true of everything that God creates, whether it be a mountain or a continent, a dewdrop or an ocean, a tree or a lion.

76

Everything having form, whether in art or nature, is the sign of an idea, and gets significance from that fact, and that only.

Whatever stands in place of an idea as its representative is called its sign, its symbol. It may be an object, a color, an odor, a taste, a movement, a gesture, a sound, a word. It may suggest the idea by its inherent character or by conventional agreement. As an example of the former, the word *rush* by its sound suggests the idea and the action for which it stands; the same is true of the words cluck, buzz, thrush, sneeze, etc. As an example of the latter, see the words in this sentence. A slight likeness of meaning suggests an object as a sign or symbol of an idea. In this way the square became the symbol of integrity; the chain, of fellowship; the dove, of innocence; the egg, of life; the eye, of frankness. By virtue of its relationship the part is able to symbolize the whole, as a sail the ship; a chimney, a house; a hand, the body; so the cause symbolizes the effect, as a match, a fire; a drought, short crops; a runaway horse, danger; so an instrument symbolizes an action, as the sword, war; the pen, peace; cordage and anchor, commerce; the retort, science. Each has its true meaning only as the idea for which it stands is apprehended. Accidental association often gives an object great power as a symbol. The cross thus became the symbol of Christianity; the garter, of a great order of knights; the crescent, of the Ottoman Empire. By its intimate relationship with the everyday life of a people, a plant or a flower becomes the symbol for a nation, as the shamrock for Ireland; the thistle for Scotland; the rose for England; the lily for France; the lotus for Egypt.

Ideas rise from objects. Engrossed with the former, we forget that the office of the latter is to serve as symbols, as tangible expressions of that which existed in another mind. Objects have no other right to be. While at first all the elements of an object must be apprehended through the senses before its full meaning can be understood, it soon happens, as a result of association and familiarity, that one element is sufficient to enable the mind to apprehend the whole object and get its full meaning. As an illustration, the odor is sufficient to call up the full picture of the rose; the taste, of an apple; the voice, of a friend; the ears, of a rabbit; a feather, of an ostrich; a letter, of a word. All of the foregoing depends upon the principle of symbolism. The wiser one becomes, the deeper and wider becomes the meaning of every sensuous element, the less dependent is he upon his sensations, for each sensation increases in symbolizing power—that is, in power to stand as the representative of other sensations and corresponding meanings. I hear the ringing of a bell, and instantly there comes to my mind the eye picture of a bell, its shape, its material, its size, and also of the word bell. I hear the word *bell* pronounced, and I at once image the sound of a bell, together with the other qualities just mentioned, and possibly also image the written or printed word bell, and probably also the muscular movement necessary to write it.

The sound of the bell or of the word bell may also stimulate the imaging of the building in which it is located, its use, its history, etc. You probably now understand what was meant by one sense symbolizing another, and how it happens that in simply tasting an object you are able to tell its shape, its texture, and its color, qualities that can come directly only through touch and sight; that in simply looking at an object you are able to tell whether it is smooth or rough, far or near—qualities and relations that originally came through touch and muscular sensation only. You must also see in this the incalculable value of symbols in all knowledge-getting. They vastly multiply the mind's power of attaining knowledge both in rapidity and comprehensiveness.

The term symbol is often used of objects having a profound meaning or relationship, in many cases far beyond the understanding of the uninitiated or of the average mind. The symbolisms of mythology, of some systems of religion, or of philosophy, reveal their beauty only to those who make them objects of special study. It is also used in other ways, but for our present purpose these uses ought not to be confounded with the use as explained in the preceding paragraphs.

If the function of all concrete, sensuous material is now clear, then everything you see about you is aglow with meaning, everything has a story to tell you. It is a principle easily recognized in psychology that an idea can be communicated from one mind to another only by giving it some physical existence, which in turn the receiving mind idealizes or interprets. The sensuous world has another function, however, than that of merely serving as the repository of an idea or a group of ideas. It through the nervous organism stimulates mental activity and invites interpretation. There is nothing that remains silent. Everything knocks at the portals of the mind through some of the senses and clamors for recognition. It catches the rays of the sun and hurls them into the eye, saying, "Look at me." It swings back and forth, driving the sound waves into the ear, saying, "Hear me." It rubs against you, saying, "Feel me." It rushes into the nostrils, insisting that you smell it, and squeezes the papillæ on the back of the tongue, urging you to taste it. In these ways it forces itself into the consciousness of the child and, as already explained, there surrenders its meaning, the idea it embodies. Every time the same sensations are aroused the same idea—that is, the same meaning—arises. The sensation is that which is interpreted, and in a way is a symbol, but it is projected and so intimately associated with the object causing it that to all intents and purposes they are one. In examining a sensation which an object produces, we usually have no other thought than that we are examining the object itself. This is more true of the child, for he has not yet learned the philosophy of the process.

An idea is always general in its nature. A symbol, as an object, is individual, but in mean-

ing is general or universal. By saying that it is
universal we mean that the same meaning or the
same thought would arise in apperceiving all the
objects of the class of objects to which that particular object belongs. The power of a symbol,
then, is determined by the depth and comprehensiveness of meaning it contains for the apperceiving mind. The less of the sensuous in proportion
to the meaning it bears, the greater its ability to
serve the mind. We must not forget that nothing
has meaning which is not given it by the mind
itself, and that an object is dependent upon the
mind for its symbolizing value. Place an object
before a child, say a hat. Discover what he knows
about it. Draw now the merest outline of the hat
on the board. He will probably see nothing there
but some " curved lines." Fill up the outline a
little, and he may see nothing more. Shade and
work in details, developing relief. When the picture can hardly be distinguished from the real
hat, he exclaims, " It is a hat." Repeat the process for a few days, and he will soon learn to recognize a hat in the slightest outline you can place
upon the board. Parts of three circles,
slightly modified, symbolize not that
hat, but the whole hat tribe to him.
Long before this he had heard the
word hat, and that had served to stand in place
of the hat itself and to symbolize hats in general. Write now the word *hat* on the board,
and by the association of the spoken word, the
hat, and the picture of the hat, it serves first to
call up the particular hat, and then to symbolize

9

the idea of hats in general. It is readily seen that the mere outline has greater symbolizing power than the fully shaded picture, and that the word hat has more than either. Repeat the experiment with other objects and with other children, and note their varying abilities in interpretation. Discover why some symbols have greater meaning to some children than to others, and why some have greater meaning to all.

The age when children are able to see in a colored picture the representation of the object varies greatly. A very young child will show some interest in himself as seen in the mirror, but probably the life in the face, as shown both by expression and movement, affords the explanation of it. If the face were perfectly still, the recognition would come later. Objects in motion are always the earliest to attract the attention of the child. The interest first shown in colored pictures is due more to the presence of the color than to any appreciation of the form.

Before a child seems able to distinguish colored pictures he has by association learned the meaning of a few words, and is already using those valuable symbols. They serve a marvelous purpose in enabling him to receive or communicate an idea concerning an object when the object itself is absent. If he wishes a drink, he may go to the pitcher and try to pour out some water. In lieu of that he may simply say " drink," and the same idea is conveyed. As soon as he learns the great convenience of words as symbols, he is disposed to discard gestures as rapidly as possible, and becomes hungry for words. At first, words mean objects and actions to him, then relations and qualities, their ideal significance becoming more abstract and less sensuous until they serve as symbols of pure ideas, and not simply as representatives of objects and their phenomena.

CHAPTER XII.

LANGUAGE.

SYMBOLISM makes language possible, the whole vocabulary of a people being a great system of symbols, each the repository, the representative of a thought from which it came and for which it speaks. As already stated, many of these words originated in an effort to imitate sounds made by animals or by bodies in motion; others are purely arbitrary forms agreed upon to represent ideas. Many words that originally belonged to the former class have become so modified by long usage that their source is not recognized save by those who make language an object of special study. Many words, at first used to express sensuous feelings and ideas only, through figurative use at last serve to express the highest emotions and thoughts of the human soul.

If children who have not learned to use language were left alone, they would easily invent a language of their own, though, of course, it would contain a limited range of words as compared with the vocabulary of their parents. The impulse to expression is characteristic of every child. He is not satisfied simply with expression, but strives to express himself in such a way as to be understood by others. No matter what kind of a sound he utters or what kind of a gesture he makes, if he finds himself understood by some one else he adopts that sound or gesture to express that same idea in the future. Every child has some words or gestures of his own manufacture which he finds profitable to use even after he has learned by imitation the words and gestures used by his associates.

A child at my table one day, when thirsty, uttered a sound resembling the caw of a tired crow, and the mother, divining its want, gave it a drink. That peculiar sound served the same purpose for many months, until by imitation it began to use the word drink. A little friend called sugar " gogo " for a year or more before she attempted to say sugar. Another habitually extended a finger toward any object he wished and closed it quickly, repeating the process with great rapidity until his wish was gratified. A little niece used the word *bum* for large, and as she learned the names of things long persisted in saying " bum-bed," " bum-apple," " bum-cat," etc. Even small children agree among themselves to call certain objects and actions by certain " made-up " names. In many cases the children agree upon some prefix or suffix to attach uniformly to all words they use, and make a language which is often difficult for adults and strangers to understand. Dr. Oscar Chrisman has gathered a mass of interesting information concerning children's secret languages, which shows how fertile are their little brains in devising vocabularies of their own.

The utility of the language spoken by those about him is so easily seen by the child that as soon as he has picked up a few words he becomes as greedy for others as the Sylene Dragon did for children to swallow. He catches them up on every hand, putting them into immediate use with such intelligence and accuracy as to surprise everybody about him. He apprehends the meaning of hundreds of them intuitively, seldom asking for their definition. I have yet to discover the child that before attempting to read has asked for the meaning of the more common conjunctions, prepositions, interjections, demonstrative pronouns, and adjectives. The meaning of many of them readily reveals itself in their concrete association, but the slight hint even thus often given shows with what insight the child is already endowed. Few children learn words in a formal way, and yet at the age of six many of them have amassed a vocabulary of from fifteen to eighteen hundred words which they can use with fair accuracy. I know a healthy child two years of age that speaks but ten words, and yet Holden reports that his son spoke three hundred and ninety-seven words at the same age. Superintendent J. M. Greenwood reports a little girl of fifteen months using sixty words, and at two years of age using five hundred. The study of children's vocabularies is one of the most fascinating and instructive phases of our subject. The following conclusions may be verified in a few weeks of investigation:

1. That after children have learned a few dozen words they readily appropriate the new

words they hear, recalling them as needed, without having made any apparent effort to remember them.

2. That children more readily understand and use such words as stand as symbols for the objects and activities with which they are surrounded, picking up relation words with similar ease.

3. That while children of the same age vary greatly in the number of words in their vocabularies, they seem to have a sufficient number to express their ideas, showing that their knowledge and vocabularies grow at approximately the same rate, and revealing also the function of language in knowledge-getting.

4. That children learn words used of objects or actions present much more readily than when they hear them read out of books or used in stories.

5. That almost without exception children who hear good English at home make few grammatical mistakes, but soon fall into grievous errors on associating with other children or with adults whose speech is faulty.

I have been surprised at the purity of the diction of some very small children. It was as chaste and appropriate as that of an Irving or a Goldsmith, there being no affectation nor stiffness, no high-sounding phrases nor cumbrous words about it. Years ago I made the acquaintance of two little boys who were talking like philosophers, using words of Latin and Greek origin with daring assurance. I discovered the explanation in the fact that their father was a man of few words, and that their mother used Anglo-Saxon only when some word of foreign extraction was not at hand. She encouraged the boys to go to the dictionary for words to use rather than to their associates. Both of them were slow thinkers and measured talkers. I recently met a boy of eleven in the mountains whose home had been there since childhood, and found him wonderfully versed in the geology of the locality, using technical terms with an ease that would give him a hearing in an academy of science.

As already remarked, children seldom lack for words to express their ideas. This is particularly true of children of from three to twelve years of age. The confusion and hesitancy of the youth is not generally found earlier in life. Children either tell what they know or frankly say they do not know. They may often be wrong in what they say, but if they think they know a thing they usually have a word for it. If these things be true, the cultivation of a child's language in these earlier years—years in which we have been exalting sense-perception—needs to be given greater prominence than is now accorded it. Nearly one fourth of his life in the public schools is spent on grammar, and when that subject is finished he talks and writes with no more ease, comparatively speaking, than when he took up the study. Grammar is too often taught as a means of helping a child correct his language, whereas proper guidance in those years when he was learning language as naturally as he was learning to walk would have made all such work unnecessary.

It is a great error to suppose that the child

learns to use words intelligently by imitation. He pronounces them by imitation, and uses them in a mechanical way as he has heard others use them; but unless their significance is apprehended, they are soon cast aside and forgotten. Words become a part of his mental furniture, his mental organism, or they prove of little service. The child has no more use for words without meaning than he has for dolls without heads. Words have meaning only as they symbolize that which he knows. If the knowledge and the word are both born in the same experience, they are indissolubly bound together thereafter. They can not be forced upon the child without doing violence to his nature, making him constrained and artificial. This serves to indicate not only the way in which words become a part of the child, but also the classes of words which he should be expected to master. Experiment with several children and note their inability to cope with abstract terms, however small, and yet how quickly they appropriate large words if they but express a familiar idea or an idea which their past knowledge or capacity now enables them to comprehend. Difficulty in pronunciation may cause a child to avoid or discard a word, hence the simpler and more euphonious vernacular forms are better suited to him. Many words are understood by small children long before they attempt to use them, as will easily be noted by any observer.

There comes a time in the child's life when words serve a greater purpose than merely to express or communicate ideas of things present.

They serve also as blocks by means of which a past experience is rebuilt or an imaginary one described. It is then that their symbolic value is more evident, for they now represent mental pictures instead of physical objects and activities. This new step in the use of language is fraught with weighty moment for the child. If with a few words he can recall the details of a past experience, locating it in time and space, he must also have taken a great step forward in mental activity. Test some of your younger children and see—

(1) What proportion of them readily recall the details of some occurrences of the week before;

(2) Whether the children with the larger vocabularies are as active and accurate as the others.

Describe some interesting scene in your own life, and make similar tests. In both cases you will find that some children who do not lack words in describing what is present to the senses are surprisingly helpless in attempts to describe what they see in the mind as an image only. If possible, discover the cause. It may simply be lack of experience; it may be something else. Whatever it is, the need for intelligent, sympathetic guidance in the transition is clear enough. Words and mind must work in as close alliance here as in sense-perception.

As the child judges and reasons, his language must serve him another purpose. You have noticed how difficult it is to get many children to compare objects or pictures directly present before them, particularly when the qualities are not very prominent or very clearly defined. When, however, the absent objects are held before the mind by means of their names only, the difficulty is multiplied many times over. Here words serve their highest function, and the success of the child in loading them up with meaning is profoundly tested.

The transition from the use of words applied to individual objects to their use in designating classes of objects or of activities is often easily made by children, and yet some of them accomplish it very slowly and very laboriously. The use of particles and of inflections to distinguish number and gender puzzles them seriously at times. Amusing mistakes of both kinds are frequently related of the children in every household at family reunions. The blunders in the use of synonyms and homonyms are exceedingly common among children who hear language a little above their comprehension, or who are required to commit passages to memory without understanding their meaning. The following illustrate them: A little friend of mine was given the text, "The Son of man came into the world not to be ministered unto but to minister." She went off repeating it to herself, and returned in a few moments, surprising her monitor by saying, "The Son of man came not to be preachered unto but to preacher." "A double-minded man is unstable in all his ways" was, after a similar effort, announced as follows, "A double-minded man is in the stable all the time." Another little sprite in the same family who had heard "The Goblins" recited attempted it herself, and where the boy

quickly dons his " roundabout " she assuringly as-
serted that he put on his " whereabouts." A study
of these movements in the language of the child
will not only prove interesting in themselves, but
will be fruitful of suggestions in a pedagogical
way.

The various transitions in the use of language
already mentioned are more or less critical stages
in the child's mental development, but the step
by which he also grasps the words as eye pictures
is no less critical. That a few straight lines and
curves having no characteristic common with the
objects they symbolize should have meaning as
well as the spoken word is as much of a marvel
to every child as it was to the Indians who held
Captain John Smith prisoner. In these days of
reading and writing, the learning of both by the
children is taken as a matter of course by parents
and teachers, but so much in their intellectual life
is dependent upon the method by which it is accomplished that it becomes at once one of the
greatest problems that confront the teacher. Our
limitations prevent further discussion here, but
we hope not further inquiry and study on the
part of the reader.

On language as related to muscular control,
see the latter part of the next chapter.

CHAPTER XIII.

MUSCULAR OR MOTOR CONTROL.

THE nerves controlling the voluntary muscles of the body lie everywhere in pairs, one for the right and one for the left side. Branching off from the spinal cord, they divide and subdivide into delicate filaments that reach even the minutest muscles of the body. They parallel the sensory nerves, which carry information of peripheral disturbance to the brain. Through them the movements of all the organs are directed. As accurate information concerning the stimuli that arouse sensation is dependent upon the healthy and prompt action of the sensor or afferent nerves, so intelligent and effective motor control is dependent upon similar conditions in the motor or efferent nerves. The earlier movements of the child are due almost entirely to reflex action, many of them serving useful ends in its physical economy. Their automatic nature is easily shown when the child has reached the stage of development in which it begins to direct the same movements by its own will, for much of the inborn skill, having served its purpose, then suddenly disappears, and control is regained only by intelligent and patient practice.

Whatever may be the mystery of connection between the mind and the nervous system, this much is clear, that the fact of such a connection can not be denied. It is also clear that this wonderful mechanism of the human frame becomes responsive to the demands of the will only through education and training. Purely reflex impulses may throw the head and arms and body and legs about in a promiscuous way, satisfying the physical cravings for activity, but the putting of a hand or a foot in a certain chosen spot is a very different thing. "Making both ends meet"—that is, grasping the toes—for the first time is a great feat in motor control. The movements of the facial muscles in taking food or crying or smiling have little of the purely voluntary element in them until they are used for a purpose more or less definitely outlining in the mind of the child. When any movement comes clearly into the consciousness of the child as of his own origination and direction, he has leaped beyond the bonds of the mere animal and already entered into the realms of spiritual existence; he is already building ideals and realizing them; the wisest man on the earth can do no more. By these movements and their accompanying sensations he gradually differentiates himself from the outside world, and discovers himself and it as having mutually independent existences: the one moving at his will, the other fixed and stable.

For lack of space we can not tarry over the multitude of interesting experiments in motor control which the child makes in the first months of his life, though they would throw much light upon the problem later on. A knowledge of the details of the structure of muscles in general and of their functions is necessary to its proper apprehension, and it might be well to refresh the memory a little before proceeding further. The motive power originating all muscular movement is physical impulse, which has been well defined as *felt pressure to activity.* That "felt pressure" may arise wholly from the accumulation of surplus nervous or muscular energy which seeks to discharge itself in exercise of some kind or as a reflex movement in response to some external stimulus, or it may arise from the presence of some thought, some idea, in the mind which awakens a mental impulse to its realization. This mental impulse in some magic way arouses a physical impulse, and the condition for action is at once attained.

The purely physical origin of the impulse is, of course, more marked in the growing child than later in life. His whole organism is set up as with compressed springs. A full-grown, vigorous man is forced into the little space the child now occupies, and he must expand to that man's stature and that man's adroitness and skill. For that purpose he eats and sleeps and exercises; for it he crams every little cell in his body with nourishment until it is alive with energy. No wonder he rolls and runs and jumps and tumbles and pulls and pushes and twists from the moment he opens his eyes in the morning until he is put to bed at night. He can not help it. He ought not to help it. It is natural with him. That is the way he grows. He is kneading himself as a woman kneads dough, and for practically the same purpose. That which he eats must be mixed through and through him, losing itself in him and becoming a part of him. The excellence of both bread and child depends upon the thoroughness of the kneading. The energy with which the child is constantly charging thus fulfills its mission.

Study the children in your circle and jot down your conclusions concerning the physical and mental condition of those whose impulses to exercise are freely indulged and of those who are inclined to exercise but little.

Whether the impulse is of physical or mental origin, its direction and control belong to the intellect. Whether the child is crawling or rolling or walking or reaching out his hands as he has something more or less clearly in mind for which he is trying to reach or which he is trying to do, he calls certain muscles into action which he thinks will accomplish that end. The knowledge of the muscles to use and the skill to control them come through a long course of experimentation. At his first voluntary efforts to reach out to something the child bends over with his whole body, instead of extending his hand alone, often losing his balance and doubling up in a helpless heap. As he tries to crawl, the same thing occurs. In both cases certain instinctive impulses to protection throw out the arms and hands and legs and feet, one or all, to little practical purpose at the time it may be, but revealing at least vaguely to the child their function and use. A few such experiences add sufficiently to the child's knowledge to start him to experimenting with them, and he soon learns how to move them independently of each other, and also how to move them together at his will. Spend a short time each day for a few weeks with a little child, and see how he learns to suppress certain superfluous and obstructive movements and to develop others that serve his purpose. Watch him as he takes hold of an object, as a pencil, as he tries to lift a spoonful of food to his mouth, as he balances himself by his chair and essays to walk, as he attempts to pronounce a word he hears you speak, as he is doing the multitude of little things which his ever-changing moods suggest to him. Compare his movements with those of other children of similar age, and, if possible, find the reason for the differences you may discover.

Your observations will show you that some children are more active than others; that some of the sluggish ones move with great precision, while some of the active ones are always blundering; that some use three or four times as much energy in doing certain things as others; that some seem to lose all control of their muscles at times, while others are never disconcerted; that the movements of the whole arm or the whole leg are gradually broken up into movements of the forearm, the hand, the fingers, the lower leg, the foot, the toes, just as the movements of the whole body were broken up into those of its larger parts; that with practice the movement in all cases be-

10

comes more and more definite; that less and less
stimulus is required to incite activities as control
becomes more complete; that the clearer the idea
in the mind of the child of what he wishes to do,
the more readily he accomplishes it; that with
each repetition a movement is the more easily
reproduced, and soon becomes almost automatic;
and that emotional and physical control grow approximately together. For the purpose of verifying these and discovering additional facts, ask
the children to thread a needle, draw a straight
line, walk a chalk line on the floor, touch the
thumb with one finger, and then move the other
fingers on the same hand independently, etc.

You never had any doubt that muscular control is to be learned by every child, but ere you
have half finished the experiments suggested you
have probably discovered that muscular control
may be greatly aided by education, and also that
there is much to learn about conducting the operation. Not only is the healthy and symmetrical
development of the child dependent upon it, but
his ability to execute the varied and delicate movements demanded in the attainment of skill in all
physical activity. Grace in standing or sitting or
walking is attained only by muscular control in
accordance with ideal standards. It comes in
many cases slowly and laboriously, but early and
intelligent instruction will greatly facilitate its
acquirement. For details consult some good authority on physical exercises for children. This
is a good place, however, to say that no forcing
process will avail. Nature never gets in a hurry.

We can furnish conditions; she does the rest.
Learn a lesson from the fields. Some of the most
graceful animals in them were the most ungainly
in their infancy. Physical constitution must affect progress in physical control, and the attempt
so often made to compel uniformity in children's
movements can but result in distortion and medi-
ocrity. It is well known that many children are
easy and natural in their movements until some
fatal day self-consciousness suddenly develops,
and the consequent embarrassment sadly inter-
feres with self-control. A word in sport, un-
friendly criticism, consciousness of inferiority or
superiority, slight physical indisposition, failure
in something attempted, lack of confidence in
self, etc., are among the causes producing it. I
once knew a child who, because of a mishap in
his first effort to walk, did not attempt it again for
nearly a year. Another alarmed her parents because after an evident effort to talk at the usual
time she remained dumb until nearly three years
of age. Imagine their relief when one day she
broke out like a magpie, astounding them all by
the accuracy and fluency of her utterances! In
this educative process, as in every other, sympathy and encouragement are two essentials.

When you reflect that gesture, speech, drawing, writing, vision, facial expression, and all manual dexterity, in addition to the movements already mentioned, depend upon perfect muscular
control, its relation to the art and the artisan side
of life becomes clear enough. Too often physical
control means simply suppression of impulses.

This is the negative side only. Its positive and practical side is seen in every effort which man makes to accomplish work, whether in the way of moving a part or all of himself or of shaping and molding something external to himself. There are a hundred and fifty thousand words in the English language alone, and yet in sound they are easily distinguished. As each one of them can be pronounced only by making its characteristic combination of muscular movements in the vocal organs, the question of motor control as related to language rises at once to a dignity scarcely less than that of thought control itself. That the child by a few years' experimenting can place these muscles under such control as to enable him to make instantly the combination necessary to produce a sound he has just heard is cause for perpetual wonder. He learns much by pure imitation, but only the larger muscular movements in speech can be learned that way. All the fine shades of tone and volume and accent can be produced only as he learns by experimentation the corresponding shades of muscular movement.

Sound utterance calls at once into requisition the delicate muscles of the vocal cords, the muscles controlling the form of the mouth and the movements of the lips and the muscles regulating respiration. Vocal expression in speaking, reading, and singing is dependent upon the ease and skill with which all of these muscles are controlled. The sensitiveness and delicacy of their response is in proportion to the fineness and mobility of their structure. Both are attained by patient and intelligent cultivation. By it the ear pictures of certain sounds become so intimately associated with their counterparts, the muscular pictures, that the presence of the former in the mind instantly and without effort accurately calls back the latter. Successful voice culture always has this for its end. Faulty articulation, stammering, lisping, lack of force, unpleasant quality, wrong pitch, etc., are generally due to inability to control properly the muscles named. The remedy has already been named, but it must be remembered that the fault may lie in the ear picture and not in the muscular picture. My friend, Professor Jones, tells me that he frequently has pupils in his classes who persist in singing flat or sharp, and that he requests them not to sing at all until they can sing the correct note. Sometimes they are silent for several days, and all at once they sing in perfect accord with the others. It is probable that during the *interim* they have been more or less unconsciously trying to produce the corresponding muscular movement as they have been correcting the ear picture of the sound. In reading and in singing by note, the eye picture and the muscular picture must be equally suggestive and interchangeable. The sight of the word or note instantly sets the machinery in motion to utter it. Long practice is just as necessary here as in the other case. This is the explanation of the inability of some people to sing by note who readily sing " by ear." The explanation is scientifically correct, for they have learned to sing by fitting their muscular movements to the ear and not to the eye picture. It is for the same reason that one person plays on the violin or other musical instrument by ear or by eye (note) only; the muscles of the hand and arm are trained to respond to but one class of mental pictures, and are helpless in the presence of the other.

Muscular control easily falls into grooves, and into very narrow grooves, too. The good penman may not be able to do anything in drawing. He may write vertically with dispatch and elegance, but make a poor scrawl in " natural slant." A good artist may be a poor penman. A fluent speaker of the German language may never succeed in pronouncing an English word correctly. One may be able to play beautifully on the piano, and yet scarcely play Old Hundred on the organ so that it will be recognized.

All physical education includes muscular control. To secure the best results for the children, the exercises should be both of a class and of an individual character: the former to meet general, the latter, individual needs. Lack of ability to perform certain movements may be due to weakness as well as to lack of control. Certain muscles may be behind their companions in development, and hence may need special cultivation.

It is not within the province of our plan to enter into details concerning motor control in the various arts, however interesting the subject might be. Manual training embraces penmanship, drawing, modeling, the use of tools in general, each leading up to useful and gainful occupations, requiring the ready command of all the voluntary muscles, particularly those of the arms and fingers. As success in life is to be so largely dependent upon the deftness and endurance of arms and fingers, every child is entitled to the education that insures both. Dexterity in any of the arts is best attained by anticipating them in childhood and youth, when the whole organism is awaiting direction, and when it easily responds to treatment. In later life form and movement are fixed, changes being made with difficulty; hence training makes little progress, and rare skill seldom results. It is on this account that motor control assumes such importance in childhood; for this reason that methods of teaching the subjects mentioned so vitally affect the future as well as the present well-being of the child. Movement and muscular control are the only things worth striving for in his earlier years; the finished product will come in its proper time. All exercises in penmanship and drawing which cramp the fingers or interfere with the free movement of the muscles do more harm than good. In every case the larger and freer movements should come first, the finer and the more restricted later. This is the law of all control. That children in the lower grades write well is not necessarily a compliment to the teacher. I have seen several children who were beautiful penmen at eight or ten years of age, and yet at twelve or fourteen were such scrawlers that they could hardly read their own writing. Finger exercises on the piano, the organ, the typewriter, and other instruments must be in accord with the laws governing the development of physical control, as many poor children have learned to their sorrow and at great expense of time and labor.

We have said that by experience the proper muscular movements for doing certain things become pictured in the mind the same as pictures furnished by the eye and the ear, and that they become so intimately associated with one or both of the latter that they mutually suggest each other. The cause of this suggestion is found in the fact that the association has made them parts of the same experience, the same whole, the same picture. At first, the intellect and will are required to direct the movement, but with repetition attention becomes less and less necessary, and both are left free to think and plan while the movement goes on to completion. As an illustration, I am now writing the words in this sentence; as I start to write each one of them, I am thinking about what word to write next, but the muscular movement necessary to write each continues "of its own accord" until the word is finished. So complete has become the alliance *that the self in thought and the self in action are one and the same thing.* This is the ideal in all motor training, particularly on the art and the artisan side. It is a mistake to suppose that in learning to write words the eye picture is the only one that must be clearly defined. The muscular picture by which each is written is just as important, and when the child has made it as fully a part of himself as the eye picture he is in no danger of misspelling it; hence the importance of accuracy and rapidity on the part of the children as they learn to write words.

That muscular control is dependent upon the condition of the nervous system is easily seen in any child; indeed, the organization of the muscular system carries with it the organization of the nervous system also. Every vital function, every activity of the body is controlled and regulated by it. Destroy the nerves, and the life of the tissue is destroyed also. Muscular control implies brain control as well. To secure the happiest results physical culture, contrary to the method so generally in vogue, should begin at the nerve centers and work outward. With intelligent exercise nerves grow in responsiveness as well as in sensitiveness and delicacy. But as the nervous system is the immediate servant of the mind, the nerve centers are best reached through it. Dr. C. W. Emerson says: " Certain mental states produce definite effects upon the vocal organs. Induce such states of mind as shall produce the desired effect in vocal expression. The mental states operate directly through the cranial nerves upon the vocal organs, and instantaneously change their activity."

Feelings and will as related to motor control will be considered in the next two chapters. For the relation of play, see the chapter on that subject.

CHAPTER XIV.

THE FEELINGS.

THE state of the self produced by the excitation of the nerves is called sensation. The action of the waves of light produces the sensation of sight; the waves of sound, the sensation of hearing, etc. All these sensations are called feelings. They are feelings, however, whose origin is purely sensuous. As was explained in a former chapter, the mass of physical feelings or sensations with which the child is constantly filled constitutes in large measure his conscious self. Feelings are the internal side of the self. They are the self alive internally with movement. As the pulse-beats are the sign of the existence of the physical life, so the feelings are the sign in consciousness of the existence of the mental life. They are always forcing themselves into consciousness as a whole, making the tone or temperament of the child, and as individuals demanding particular attention to the exclusion of others. Feelings are purely mental states in distinction from mental activities. These "states" are, however, *internal* activities. They bear in a general way the same relation to the mental activities of thought and will that cellular activities do to muscular activities. Without the first in either case the other could not arise.

The second class of feelings is called emotions. They are produced by the presence of some thought in the mind. Their origin is wholly mental. They accompany all intellectual activity and owe their characteristics to it as sensations owe their characteristics to the nature of the physical stimulus. As some sensations are pleasurable and others painful, so also are the emotions. Both get their agreeable or disagreeable character from their harmony or lack of harmony with the self. If in harmony, satisfaction and pleasure result; if out of harmony, the opposite. Sensations precede the thought, and are that out of which the mind gets meaning or thought. Emotions rise as the idea comes, and may be said to follow it. Hold an apple before a child; the sensation of sight occurs, and he interprets it as that of an apple; immediately an emotion of pleasure arises. Bring him some bitter medicine; following the sensation and thought of what it is comes a feeling of displeasure. He hears some one speak, and recognizes the sound as that of mother's voice; emotions of pleasure fill his soul. He hears a bark, and recognizes it as that of a dog that has bitten him; fear at once possesses him. He is expecting pudding for dinner, and mother brings him pie instead; disappointment possesses him as he sees what it is. In all these cases sensations only would result had he not given them meaning. Emotions followed only after the sensations were interpreted.

Sensations always mingle more or less with emotions, each enhancing the pleasure or pain of the other according as they happen to be in or out of accord. The sound of a voice is more pleasing to the child as there mingles with it the emotion arising from the discovery that it is mother's voice. The bark of the dog suddenly becomes harsh as the child discovers that it is that of the biting dog instead of his own little pet, as he had supposed. A keepsake is more gratifying to the eye than its mate of the same material and form because of the emotions it begets. For this reason children's emotions and interests are aroused most readily by poetry and music. The jingle of words, the rapid recurrence of rhythm and rhyme, and the abrupt changes in movement, pitch, and volume excite sensations, sustain the attention, and quicken the emotions. *Hey diddle, diddle, the cat and the fiddle*, has far more pleasure and interest for the child than *the cat and the violin*. *Rock-a-bye baby upon the tree top* would have died the day it was born had there been only the motion of ordinary prose in it.

Children's emotions usually reveal themselves in nervous activity of some kind. It does not take an expert to read a child's feelings in the expression on his face, the light of his eye, or the movements of his hands and arms. Only as a child learns to dissemble can he repress the revelation. In some children, as you will see by observation, the sympathy between the nervous system, both vegetative and cerebro-spinal, is much more intimate and responsive than in others.

A little nephew of mine had such a telltale countenance that even the slightest shades of emotion
were constantly expressing themselves in the ever-
changing lights and shadows that played over his
face. His complexion was as pure and clear as
truth itself, and the freshness of each returning
blush made me feel that I was nearer the actual
soul of the child than I had ever been before.
Wonder, pleasure, doubt, confidence, fear, anger,
surprise, humor, embarrassment, annoyance, disappointment, weariness, supplanted each other in
quick succession, outrivaling in variety and beauty
the rarest combinations of tints that the most cost-
ly kaleidoscopes unfold. Discover how many of
the children in your circle are "so nervous"
that they become perceptibly or violently agitated
as any of the above-named emotions arise; note
how the agitation expresses itself. Classify the results in each case, and, if possible, discover the
cause. In fright, some will blush and some will
blanch. Why? Discover how the emotions affect
appetite, digestion, respiration, circulation, sleep,
motor control in general, etc.

In your investigations you will find that the
well-balanced emotional nature is usually a sign
of a healthy, well-balanced physical organism, re-
affirming the idea of their interdependence and
emphasizing the importance of everything that has
been said concerning the care and development of
the body of the child. You will doubtless also
discover that you have often dealt unjustly with
children because of your lack of knowledge of this
fact; that often the very evil you had been try-

ing to cure had but been grievously aggravated by the methods you had pursued. Experiment now in controlling the emotions of the children by giving them appropriate things to think about, and note how promptly physical agitation subsides as some gentler emotion replaces a violent or an unpleasant one.

Many interesting reports have been published on inquiries made concerning the presence and origin of the different emotions in the child, and you will be pleased to make similar investigations in your circle. They seem to show in a general way that many children are entirely devoid of fear even after they enter their teens, and that a small per cent grow into manhood and womanhood without knowing what fear is save by hearsay; others display fear when but a few months old. The emotion of fear is a stranger to some children until a serious accident has happened to them or their friends, and then they become very timid. Some fear animals, others ghosts, others burglars, others thunder and lightning, others father and mother, others a steam engine, a bridge, water, death, a gun, ridicule, darkness, etc. One colored girl reports to a friend of mine that she fears nothing except a feather! Each of the emotions afford abundant data in similar variety. They all throw a flood of light upon the course to be pursued in the care and management of the child.

You are referred to works more advanced for a full discussion of the various classes of emotions. Emotions may get their characteristics from the relation of the experience to the present time; those arising from a present experience may be called *immediate;* from recalling a past experience, *retrospective;* from looking forward to a future experience, *prospective.* They may get their general characteristics from the objects awakening them, as personal and impersonal. The personal emotions include the social, moral, and religious emotions; the impersonal include the intellectual and æsthetic. Some of these will be treated in independent chapters.

The third great class of feelings is the affections, or the loves and likes. Affections are to be distinguished from the two preceding classes in that they are feelings which result from the new adjustment of the self toward objects which have produced pleasing sensations or emotions. The self naturally goes out in a kindly flow of feeling toward that which produces either. Emotions and sensations are not thus projected. Love must have an object. Likes and loves are always pleasurable, reacting upon the self and intensifying the pleasure of the emotions of which they may be regarded as the overflow. Dislikes and hates are the result of painful sensations and emotions, and the flow of feelings is away from rather than toward that which causes them. Likes and loves identify the self and the object in interest. Dislikes and hates hold them apart. Likes and loves wish well and take pleasure in the well-being of their objects as they do of themselves. Dislikes and hates wish ill and take pleasure in the misfortunes of their objects—persons or things.

Children respond in loves and likes with surprising promptness. They very early show a preference for the nurse who handles them so tenderly and hums to them so softly, as well as for the food that gratifies their palate and allays their hunger. Many a mother has found it extremely difficult to displace a nurse in the affections of her child, because the bias had already been given before she was able to give him her attention. In a similar way she finds it almost impossible to get him to eat a different kind of food from that which he has already learned to like. Subterfuges and imitations with no end of coaxing are necessary in many cases to overcome antipathy for other foods. A few sticks of candy, a merry romp, a buggy ride, a kind word in time of need, will, as any one knows, quickly kindle a child's love for the giver. That children's affections are very fickle and are easily transferred is probably due as much to lack of memory in the new pleasure as to anything else. Where the kindly treatment has been of long continuance, however, the affection even in very young children is not so easily disturbed as many people imagine.

If you will make inquiries concerning the children in your circle, you will find many interesting facts pertaining to the origin, development, and extinction of likes and loves. You will see on what slight provocation an affection may spring up and how intense it may be for a few days or weeks, and then how suddenly it may disappear. In some cases the cause of the affection may be discovered at once, and in others no special reason may show itself. Be sure to note the things which most easily arouse the affections of children, and what changes take place in their preferences as they grow older. Some children will be found to possess little or no affection in the true sense of the word, while others respond generously to every force that touches them kindly.

Loves may be classified according to their objects, as love of kindred, love of friends, love of home, love of country, love of society, love of property, love of power, love of action, love of knowledge, love of truth, etc., each having a variety of subdivisions which may readily be discovered by you. The undue preponderance of one of these or the absence of any one of them in a child should raise at once an inquiry concerning its cause.

The fourth class of feelings is called *desires.* Your investigations have shown you that the children not only love that which contributes to their pleasure and happiness, but that an impulse to possession, to the assurance of the continuance of that object in its present relations to them, is also usually present in some degree.

Such an impulse is called a *desire.* Love responds more or less blindly to its stimulus, which is also true of desires in the earlier stages of the child's life. Then its impulsive character is more prominent; but later its object is selected with some discrimination, and its intellectual side appears. On account of the close relationship of the desires and affections, the classes of both are practically the same. Appetites are physical desires. Desires are satisfied in the sensation or

11

emotion which their gratification begets. By experience the child learns what objects or classes of objects produce certain sensations and emotions, and he very early begins the regulation of his desires in accordance with that knowledge. Such regulation is naturally directed to physical desires first, and next to those of a higher order. Desires whose gratification produce pain, or less pleasure than others, are repressed, or subordinated to those whose satisfaction insures him greater enjoyment. He suppresses a desire for the time being, that its gratification may be more complete in the future. Gradually physical desires and those relating to the self alone become subordinated to the moral desires and to those affecting the pleasure and happiness of his fellows. This process of organizing the desires and its reactive effect on the character of the child will be treated further in the chapter on the Will.

CHAPTER XV.

MOTOR control has already been explained. The physical impulse furnishes the motive power for all muscular activity. As there is no motion in the steam engine without steam, so there is no motion in the body without the impulse. As the engineer directs the steam in the engine, so the intellect guides the power arising in the impulse to the execution of certain specific movements. These two elements, physical impulse and intellect, constitute the will in all voluntary bodily activity.

Will is simply the self originating and directing its own activities. The initiatory movement is always found in impulse; the selecting and directing, in the intellect. The intellect fixes upon some end to reach, some particular movement to execute, some work to perform, and regulates the motive power of the impulse in such a way as to accomplish it effectively.

The body is under control when it responds easily and promptly to the demands which the intellect makes upon it. This concrete will action, which begins in a very simple way with the child, gradually organizes and brings under control the

115

entire locomotive machinery of the body, including impulses and the muscular and nervous systems. While he is thus gaining control of his
physical powers, his mental impulses are also slowly rising into consciousness and re-enforcing the
physical impulses. The latter differentiate into
well-defined appetites or physical desires, while the
former as clearly objectify and become distinct
mental desires. So largely are bodily and mental
activities moving together in the earlier years of
the child's life that the control of the former
means practically also the control of the latter.
His mental life differentiates from his physical
life very slowly. Each serves and strengthens the
other as the former is attaining that high position in which it alone is to be master. In the
process physical appetites and desires gradually
become subordinated to mental desires, and prudential and moral control begin to define.

Desires are impulses directed toward objects
which it is thought will give pleasure or profit.
Impulses, as pure *felt pressure*, are not consciously
directed toward any object or class of objects.
Through experience the child recognizes in a general way at least the character of the impulse, and
recalls objects which once satisfied it. Naturally
he sets them up for consideration, and the impellent force carries him toward one, then toward another, possibly toward all, often producing puzzling confusion. This is what is called conflict or
clash of impulses or desires. The child determines
the question of preference by estimating the varying abilities of the different objects to satisfy the

generic impulse out of which the desires have risen. He selects that one which in his judgment possesses the greatest power, and all of the impellent forces press toward it, the different impulses and desires yielding at once to that one which was in the line of the choice just made. Many things affect the estimate and the choice; the child's former experiences, his education, his environments, his needs, the advice of others, etc.

The choice once made, the desire is re-enforced by the new impulse resulting from the conscious possibility of satisfaction, and thus motive power for its realization is supplied. In all the movement thus far feeling and intellect have been reacting upon each other for the purpose of fixing definitely upon the end to be attained and in clearing the deck for action. These things being done, it now remains for the mind to select the means by which the end is to be realized. The factors that control the selection of ends also control the selection of means. Suppose the desire be for a drink: a glass of water being near, the impulse is directed through the muscles of the arm for bringing the glass to the mouth. If it be to divide an apple, the impulse, under similar direction in each case, moves the hand to the pocket for a knife, both hands open it, and both are used in performing the operation. If it be to utter a certain word, the impulse is directed through the appropriate muscles. This final executive act of the will is called *volition*.

The above analysis shows that there are two clearly defined functions of the will: they are the idealizing and realizing functions. The will sets up the ends to be attained, and proceeds to attain them also. In the above illustrations, as in all motor control, the realizing function is dependent upon the readiness with which the physical organism responds to the directive force of the mind. The object of manual training in all its branches is to develop such perfect harmony of action between the idealizing and realizing activities or functions of the will that little or no attention need be given to the latter. As skill in any line approximates perfection, the movement becomes so nearly automatic that muscular effort is practically reduced to nothing. The mind is thus left free to attend to the formation and retention of the ideal which is realizing. The tool of the expert graver and the nimble fingers of the modeler alike work out unerringly the invisible lines which the mind busily runs for them.

The physical organism, however, is not the only part of himself which the child must control. Attention, as explained in a former chapter, is not the concentration of muscular or nervous energy, but of the mental activities. Every voluntary act of the mind is just as much an act of the will as is every voluntary physical movement. Notion building, judgment, recollection, thinking, etc., are possible only to him who controls these activities as fully as he controls the various muscles of the body. It requires an act of the will to distinguish between a pen and its holder, to put a dog and his collar together in a mental picture, to determine that one orange is larger than an-

other, to rebuild the picture of a bird seen yesterday, to discover the cause of the withering of the
rose in the vase on the table, to get the meaning
of the line—

Kind hearts are more than coronets.

Mental impulses and desires are suppressed,
subordinated, and organized in the same manner
as the physical, and the process needs little further
explanation. One of the principal things to remember is that time and practice are required in
both cases. It is the function of physical and
manual training to develop and perfect control
and skill in every bodily organ. It is the function
of education on the mental side to accomplish
the same thing for the mental activities. Freedom
in the use of the latter is just as essential as in the
use of the former. The child needs to be trained
so that he can do more than simply turn his attention to a subject to the exclusion of others. He
must attain to that power which will enable him
to bring at once to its comprehension and solution the whole of himself, his past knowledge, his
past experiences, his accumulated strength.

Control as related to the will and as thus far
considered merely places the child in possession
of himself as he may wish to serve immediate ends.
He is now, as it were, familiar with his tools, and
knows how to use them. A little inquiry, however, will show that another class of ends has been
building up out of his experience. The mastery
of his physical powers is to serve a higher purpose
than the immediate gratification of his impulses,

the awakening of pleasurable sensations and emotions. The skillful use of his mental faculties has a higher mission than the mere satisfaction which comes from their exercise. The economic value of both has already been suggested. Control saves energy and time. It insures definiteness and accuracy. It multiplies vastly the amount of work which may be accomplished. Learning from his experiences, the child sees not only that one object or action may serve him better than another, but that one of two or three or many may in the end bring him all of the profit and enjoyment that all the others could have brought. In other words, he learns not only the way to accomplish a certain end with the least expenditure of mental and physical force, but he learns also to select an end which will be the most fruitful in results.

Control thus keeps *advantage* constantly in view. It makes one end serve as a means to another. It denies itself present gratification for future gratification and profit; or, better, it finds present enjoyment in the anticipation of a future enjoyment which it sets machinery in motion to ' insure. Control organizes itself upon a *prudential* basis. Everything that the child or the man does is determined beforehand by weighing its advantage or disadvantage. He buttons up his coat collar to keep from getting a sore throat; he saves his pennies that he may buy a ball; he learns his letters that he may be able to read; he is a good boy that he may win his mother's approbation; he exercises that he may grow strong; he talks re-

spectfully to a larger boy that he may not catch a
threshing; he carries in a large boxful of wood
in the afternoon that he may not be compelled
to go out in the dark after more; he treats his
playmates kindly that they may love him; he sows
that he may reap. In all of this he gradually
learns how one thing depends upon others, and
organizes all these means so that they mutually
contribute toward higher·or more far-reaching advantage. He becomes somewhat of a business
man, working for pay, making or raising things
to sell, buying and selling, studying the laws of
production and of trade, developing insight, caution, self-denial, confidence.

The discussion thus far has probably made will
and control sufficiently clear to guide you more
fully in your observations with the children. Verify each of the statements concerning the origin
and growth of the will. Discover how largely
the younger children are creatures of impulse, and
what forces are each day conspiring to their control. What is the connection of the feelings in
general with the various kinds of control? If
any of the children have "weak wills," what is
the cause? Why do some children have good physical and intellectual control and yet lack prudence? Why do others possess the latter and lack
the others? How much may be attributed to poor
health or to home government? How much of
the control is due to outside pressure as the incentive of some reward or the fear of punishment?
How much is due to the child's own desire and
ability to realize the ideals for himself? What

physical obstacles seem to be in the way? How
far is the control natural and spontaneous? Why
are some children so far behind others? Are any
of them possessed of evil spirits, or do they simply need some loving, sympathetic, painstaking
friend to assist them in their efforts at getting
control of themselves?

This last question suggests the relationship
which wills bear to one another. They are always
affecting one another for better or for worse. The
far-reaching influence of a child's playmates,
though unconsciously directed, is known to everybody. The educational process as a whole is well
defined as *the influencing of one will by another in
a more or less methodical way in order to assist it
to an ideal development.* The education of the will,
the development of control in its many-sided
senses, is the real end and aim of all education.
The will of the child may be influenced in a purely
infectious way or by intelligent counsel and assistance. It can not be accomplished by a few
spasmodic efforts from time to time, but only by
that same slow and regular process by which Nature produces all of her rarest creations.

In the attainment of control the same law
holds as in all other mental activity. Each effort
reacts upon the child, making him stronger for
the succeeding experience. The gain each time
may be imperceptible, but at the end of a series
will manifest itself clearly enough. In that way
he goes on from strength to strength, choosing
more intelligently, more promptly, more accurately; executing more easily, more skillfully, more

effectively; becoming more resourceful, more deliberate, more self-reliant. The reaction upon the
self affects all sides of the child's emotional nature, and gives that balance and poise to the character which insures self-possession and intelligent
action even under unexpected and trying diffi-
culties.

Will reaches its highest function in moral control—that is, control of the self in accord with an
ideal of right. Pure advantage as a motive here
yields to a higher desire—that of right doing.
Some children very early distinguish between
right and wrong; others long confuse the idea of
advantage with that of right. They are apt to
think that whatever gives them or gives their
friends pleasure is right, and that whatever gives
them pain is wrong. All are moved quickly by
the incentive of advantage, particularly if the advantage is immediate, but the incentive to be true
affects many of them very slowly. The child naturally thinks more about getting and having than
about doing and being. The general movement by
which moral control is obtained is the same as that
just explained in prudential control. Its further
discussion will be found in the chapter on Manners
and Morals.

CHAPTER XVI.

THE INTELLECT AND ITS FUNCTIONS.—PERCEPTION, MEMORY, AND IMAGINATION.

CONSCIOUSNESS, apperception, and attention have been defined and explained. They are general functions of the intellect, entering as they do more or less into all mental activity. It remains to examine the special functions of *perception, memory, imagination, conception, judgment, and reasoning.* The treatment of each must necessarily be brief.

Perception is the act of getting knowledge of individual objects present to the senses. It is the *initial* stage in all apperception. It tells us simply what a thing is as present before us; gives us its form, color, texture, material, weight, surface, parts, movements—summing all up in a mental picture whose wider relations and fuller meanings are discovered by apperception proper or by comparison and reasoning. An object is lying by my paper as I write. Through perception I discover a handle, its shape, and the material out of which it is made; a long blade is attached at one end and two small blades at the other. Though I may not know its name, I have the picture of a knife clearly defined in my mind. The knowledge of any or of all of the parts together is called perception, and yet you readily see that more or less of my past experience has gone into the building up of the picture and given it the meaning it now possesses; in so far as this is true, there is a suggestion of apperception—that is, a perception to which has been *added* a meaning greater than that which lies in the object unrelated to any past experience. A second look at the knife shows me that it is mine; that it is a valuable knife; that it is of modern make; that it is fit for certain kinds of work only; all this and much more is apperceived. I once saw a lady alight from a train and fall into the arms of a company awaiting her. All were in tears and were dressed in deep black. Perception gave me this knowledge. Apperception told me that there were sorrow and mourning and death and broken hearts and vacant chairs. On the wall is a small painting. Through perception I get the form of a house, of leafless trees, of broken fences, of alternations of dark and light colors stretching away over and beyond the house, of a round white spot above, of blotches of white paint covering the roof of the house and hiding the earth from view. Through apperception I know that it is winter, that it is midnight and cold and lonely and desolate. Perception, in a word, tells us what things present are and apperception tells what they mean. The educated and the uneducated perceive things about alike, but the educated and the experienced apperceive far more in everything they meet than the others.

The laws of association and dissociation apply to perception as well as to apperception. Perception locates objects in time and space, giving them relations to one another and to the self. The process of distinguishing objects from one another and of noting the various elements that compose them and the characteristics peculiar to them, together with their resemblances, is of the utmost importance in the child's life. Its value in the intellectual life depends primarily upon its accuracy and, secondarily, upon its rapidity and many-sidedness. Sluggishness of action and narrowness of vision must ever debar the child from attaining to a wide knowledge of things. The mental side of all knowledge gained directly through the senses is perception, and much of the discussion concerning their functions and their culture should be reviewed here.

To show how apperception affects perception, several figures, some of them reproductions, are given on the opposite page. They will be found valuable as well as entertaining in experimenting with the children. As soon as the children find themselves deceived in the figures they will become very wary, and proceed with such caution that many of them can not readily be misled again. Notice the particular temperaments most generally making mistakes. Take now several small wooden balls or cubes of varying sizes, two or three of each being of the same size, and test the children's ability to distinguish among them. Some of the smaller balls or cubes should be skillfully loaded inside with shot, so as to be equal in

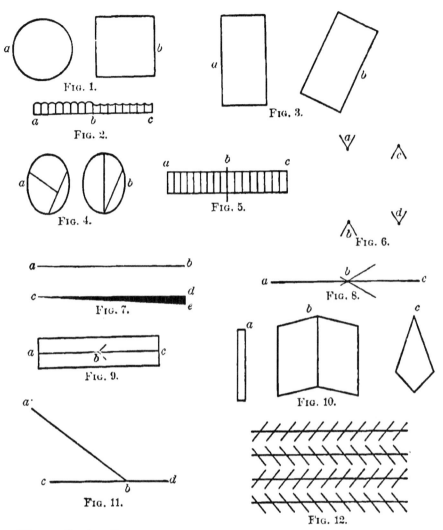

Fig. 1. Is the diameter of the circle > or < than the side of the square? Fig. 2. Which is longer, ab or bc? Fig. 3. Which of the rectangles is the longer? Fig. 4. Which horizontal diameter is the greater? Fig. 5. Which is the longer, ab or bc? Fig. 6. Which is the greater distance, ab or cd? Fig. 7. Is the line cd or the line ce parallel to ab? Figs. 8 and 9. Which is the longer, ab or bc? Fig. 10. Which is the longer, a or c? Does the book, b, open toward or from you? Fig. 11. Which is the longer, ab or cd? Fig. 12. At which end do these lines converge?

If these figures are placed on the blackboard or transferred to chart paper, they can be used with excellent success before the classes.

weight to the next larger size. See what effect the suggestiveness of size has upon the estimate of weight. Your own experience will suggest to you a number of tests serving a similar purpose.

Memory is the act of recalling the picture of a past experience. The experience must come back approximately as it occurred, and the self must recognize it as having been an experience of its own in a certain more or less definite time and place. Its value depends also upon its accuracy, its rapidity, and its comprehensiveness. Without memory there could be no progress in knowledge-getting. However valuable the presentative activities already described may be, if memory be wanting their cultivation and development are impossible. They reciprocally affect each other. Perception makes little advancement if memory is not following closely behind.

As each experience helps to an understanding of the next, the place of memory is easily enough seen. This particular function is so important that the question naturally arises whether memory ought to be made to serve any other purpose. If a past experience contains one or more elements similar to those of the present experience, the law of suggestion is usually potent enough to provoke its spontaneous recall and application to the new experience without any special effort of the mind. If you will watch the children at their plays, you will see how fully this law controls. Watch them at their house games, and see how much more readily many of them learn details than do their elders. See also how quickly an

12

experience in one line is used by the child to help him in understanding another when their similarity seems very slight even to you. Under such demands note how little repetition is necessary to enable many children to recall the aids that unlock the meaning to the new experience. Children seldom worry about remembering things. They remember them only as they creep into their consciousness by the laws already named. They do little feeling around in the past until they grow older or until the task is set before them. This great function of memory being so evident, the advantage of certain lines of sequence in the everyday experiences of the child needs no further argument. Art is thus made possible.

But memory serves another great purpose in furnishing to the self its past experiences in order that it may reason about them and discover the principles and laws involved in them, their likenesses and differences, their nature and value. You have noticed how difficult it is for some children to see the similarity or dissimilarity of two things you are talking about, particularly as they are compelled to hold one of them in the memory. The vagueness of details in the memory picture and its disposition to slip away entirely were constantly defeating you. Induction and deduction are both impossible without memory. The more readily a child recalls experiences having common elements, the more accurately and the more rapidly does he discover a body of laws and principles. Such discoveries react upon the mind, multiplying with wonderful rapidity the child's power of retention and recollection. Science and philosophy are thus assured.

Memory also serves a great end in a prudential way. Half of the misfortunes of childhood come because the child forgets what he has experienced or what has been told him. Out of memory caution quickly develops and control becomes possible. The memory of yesterday's bumping prevents another tumble downstairs to-day; of this morning's sting, the handling of another wasp; of father's displeasure, the loss of the hatchet; of last night's sore throat, exposure to cold. Not always promptly, nor with all children, do these results follow, but sooner or later they come and grow into a system with untold benefits to the individual and to society.

The pleasures of memory are not excelled by those of the imagination, of which poets so profusely sing. Childhood hours—mother's lullaby, the fragrance of the apple blossoms, the songs of the robin, the stories round the old hearthstone, the Thanksgiving dinner, the midnight visit of Kris Kringle, the little red schoolhouse in the neck of the woods, the jingle of sleigh bells, the thrill of love's first dream, the visit to Aunt Mary's, the old singing school, the old oaken bucket, the cows winding slowly o'er the lea, the night when troth was plighted, the day when we first entered a home of our own—are but a few of the multitude of beautiful visions which ever and anon drive out the care of to-day and fill the soul with happiness. Even the sorrows and struggles of the past have a halo about them that makes their remembrance dear to every heart.

In efforts at expressing thought by symbols, particularly by language, memory serves another great function. Facts, events, dates, names, places, persons, forms, colors, movements, principles, laws, must be recalled in an orderly way that the mind may carry on a connected line of thought; words with which to express the idea appropriately must also reappear at the exact time needed. Happy is the child to whom all these come spontaneously. But, generally speaking, special effort is necessary for their recall, and memory takes the form of recollection.

Recollection is memory under control and direction of the will. By utilizing the laws of association and suggestion, the will rebuilds a former experience, slowly or rapidly as the degree of familiarity may permit. By this it must not be understood that memory proper, as spontaneous, reproduces a past experience without any mental effort whatever, but simply that such effort is reduced to a minimum. Every mental state is an activity, as has been explained, memory not excepted. In recollection will and effort come into prominence in consciousness as factors. Ability to recall a part or all of an experience at will is invaluable in any occupation or profession the youth may enter.

Discover whether your children are recalling spontaneously or with evident effort; how many remember places better than names, facts better than principles; what they see better than what they hear; what interests them better than what does not; what is recent as compared with what is remote; what they understand as compared with what they do not. Find out what effect physical depression or fear has upon memory; whether they remember names better than dates, and the cause of it; what is the effect of repetition. Do they remember poetry better than prose? If so, why? Find out also whether you are not making life a burden to them in requiring them to " commit to memory " many things that would remain with them with little effort if given later on, and whether there are not many things which they could easily appropriate now that you are withholding for the future.

If your inquiries are pursued far enough, you will have material sufficient to keep you thinking for a long time. Your conclusions will prove about as follows:

The more clearly a child understands a subject,

The more it affects his personal interests and needs,

The more vivid the original impression,

The more definitely it is related to his other knowledge,

The more carefully the natural sequence is followed in approaching it,

The less will be the effort necessary for its recall. Repetition and writing as memory aids will probably take a subordinate place in your methods, though not losing their value entirely. Correct habits in knowledge-getting will seem more desirable than a great amount of knowledge itself.

Imagination is the third great notion or picture-forming activity of the intellect. *Its function is to embody the ideal in concrete forms.* Perception gives us the idea of an object. Imagination reverses the process. It starts with the idea and expresses it in some individual form. It is creative. It produces new forms. These may be constructed in a mere mechanical way, with little or no definite purpose in view, or in accord with the highest ideals of the human soul. In their origin they may be almost exclusively emotional or as exclusively intellectual. They range all the way from the laying of a few sticks together in a certain way to the carving of the Apollo Belvidere; from the potato-masher to the linotype; from "Ba, ba, black sheep" to the book of Job; from the rude hut to the towering cathedral; from the crude sketches of the simple-minded peasant to the noble frescoes of the Vatican. Out of imagination rises the beautiful world of art, inspiring and refining the race. It touches every side of life, and makes progress possible.

In its simpler and more mechanical form the imagination is largely inventive, the end being to construct something rather than to express or embody an idea, or even to produce something to serve a specific purpose. Children will often labor for hours to build a mud dam or a block house, and then destroy it in an instant without a shadow of compunction. Their plays constantly call into requisition their imaginative powers, and the marvelous freedom with which they make, destroy, burn, kill, fly, die, come to life again, become rich, lose all their property, sail to the moon, administer medicine, become grandmothers, soldiers, sailors, merchants, showmen, monkeys, dogs, cats, horses, bears, sheep, fairies, griffins, cowboys, ghosts, or angels—all in imagination—is well known to everybody. There is just as much art in all this as there is in the pictures the child draws or the models he makes from clay. This process of modifying the things he is, the things he has, and the things he sees and hears, but forecasts what he will be doing in youth and manhood. The greater the skill which he attains in putting his experiences into new forms and in devising ways and means of doing things, the better will be his preparation for active life.

Read or tell a story to the children, and discover the differences in the pictures which they form of it. Some will note every detail, others scarcely any. Ask them to tell an original story or act an original part, and note the differences among them. Give half of the girls dolls and the other half scraps of ribbons and dress goods; give half of the boys water-color paints and brushes and the other half sand pans; keep busy yourself, but watch them and see what they do. Give them curious toys, and discover who will find out first how to play with them. Give them all simple puzzles and see who will find their way out first. Show them pictures and give all a chance to tell what they see in them. Give them rings, colored sticks, colored beads, colored strips of paper, pencils, soft clay, needles and thread, etc., and see what they make out of them. Note particularly who are original and who follow others. Find where all get their ideas for the new forms. Which are more imaginative, boys or girls? Note also who seem to take more pleasure in color than in form pictures. The study will have special value if you discover the causes of the differences among the children, and note the influence which a little suggestion from you may have.

The inquiries just suggested are intended more for the smaller children, but you will readily devise methods for making appropriate tests with older children. Compare the memoranda and discover how the imagination in the different ages varies. New themes now interest them. Images form more rapidly. Delicacy and fineness begin to characterize them. They bear the stamp of individuality. Ornamentation in some cases and utility in others show the trend of emotion or thought. Have them read The Building of the Ship, The Village Blacksmith, Maud Muller, Snow Bound, and tell you the stories in their own language. Ask them to describe a certain landscape, yesterday's thunderstorm, the old mill, and note the plainness of some and the rich coloring of others. You will find some extremely practical, others visionary and fanciful; some resourceful, others wholly lacking in originality and creative power.

In its highest sense as creative, imagination seeks to produce forms that will symbolize universal ideas, with little sensuous material to ex-

press great truths. Its test is its weight of meaning; its themes, the deepest emotions of the
human heart. As the youth begins to think and
to feel deeply, he begins to catch the deeper meanings of the creations of Nature and of art, and
to long to express them himself. Lack of space
forbids elaboration, but the development of the
child's imagination from the purely mechanical
to fancy and to the higher forms of creative activity is one of the most fruitful themes for inquiry
and study.

Perception, apperception, and memory depend much upon imagination for the filling out
of the details in the mental pictures they form.
It is sometimes so active that the child is self-
deceived, for it covers up the real elements in an
object with the wealth of associated elements
which it immediately images. Memory pictures
are often most unreliable for the same reason and
because of the inability of the child to distinguish
between the old and the new elements present.
On this account children are often punished for
falsehoods for which they are not responsible, or
at most not wholly to blame.

An imagination that simply understands and
appreciates what another constructs is sometimes
called *passive*. That which constructs is called
active. The terms may help to a distinction, but
it is easily seen that all imagination is active; that
however suggestive and complete the creation of
another may be, it is still necessary for the receiving mind to construct its own picture in order to
get its meaning. The greatest painting in the

world is but a varicolored canvas to him who knows not how to give it relief and life. Even *Home, Sweet Home* has scarcely more than rhythm to him who as he reads can not construct the pictures of the palaces and their gay throngs, the thatched cottages and the humble hearth-stones, the caroling birds and the lonely exile.

Like the other picture-forming activities, imagination everywhere obeys the laws of association and suggestion, often responding to the slightest stimulus, constructing and building, combining and recombining, " turning even airy nothingness to forms and shapes " of beauty and of use. It is to this rare faculty that we owe the wealth of figures that illuminate and vivify the world of literature.

The cultivation, direction, and control of the imagination of the child demand understanding and skill of the highest order. Into its upbuilding flows every current of his mental life. Upon its genius every ideal and every destiny depend.

CHAPTER XVII.

THE INTELLECT AND ITS FUNCTIONS (CONTINUED). —CONCEPTION, JUDGMENT, REASONING.

EVERY act of the mind is more or less complex, calling into exercise as it does a variety of activities. Its name depends upon the activity most prominent in consciousness. Imagination is dependent upon memory for its materials, memory upon perception, perception upon sensation. In certain measure, also, the reverse is true, as has been explained. Apperception involves them all. The additional general intellectual processes named are conception, judgment, and reasoning.

Formerly the term conception had a twofold signification. It was used as synonymous with perception, or individual notion, and also as signifying the notion of a class. It is now fast losing the former meaning and is being used in the latter sense. It will be used here as applied to mental pictures as general notions only. Notions of classes are built up by analysis and synthesis much in the same way as notions of individual objects. As an illustration, a child meets for the first time a few dozen apples of different varieties. He examines one and finds it nearly spherical, with a positive indentation and a stem at one end and a

slight depression with rudiments of leaves at the
other.   He notes the covering, the difference in
the outside and the inner part of the flesh, the
kinds of seeds and seed cases, the texture and
taste.   He examines another, and a score of them,
and discovers that in all these things they practically agree.   Some are larger than others; some
are tart, some sweet, some mealy, some soft, others
hard.   They vary in color and a little in general shape, but the points of likeness recur so
often and are so clearly marked that they enter
into the notion or mental picture of the class
apple as a whole.   He recognizes objects as apples
only as they possess those characteristics.   A large
number of green leaves are examined.   Each leaf
is found to be flat, to possess a midrib with
branches and a network of veins, to be composed
of a pulpy cellular center, to have a stem on which
it rises from the twig, though varying greatly in
form, in margin, in thickness, and in special character of venation.   The common or like elements
are united into a mental picture of leaves in general—a picture which any ordinary leaf will fit.
If you were to mold a leaf out of clay, or cut one
out of paper, or draw a picture of one, in all cases
you would make it more or less in accord with this
general notion or picture.   What is true of the
apple or leaf is also true of the triangle, or square,
or sphere, or fish, or star, or house, or wagon, or
flower.

For the above reasons a *conception* may be defined as *an image which symbolizes the general processes by which all the individual members of the*

class to which it belongs are constructed. The conception of a triangle is that of a polygon with three sides and three angles. With that image only in the mind, you may construct ten thousand triangles, no two being alike save in the requirement of the conception—three sides and three angles. Sometimes few, sometimes many elements enter into the conception to distinguish the class from other classes. In a simple way life is the only element that enters into the conception of animate objects to distinguish them from inanimate objects; the spinal column to distinguish the class vertebrates from the invertebrates; solidity to distinguish ice from water. It is true that in each case other characteristic elements may be implied, but they follow by virtue of the existence of the ones named.

The analysis of the process just explained shows the following steps:

1. Attention to one particular element found common to all the individuals of the class, as the sphericity in the apples, the midrib in the leaves, the three angles in the triangles, life in animate beings, etc.

2. The comparison of the element as discovered in the individual members of the class and of other classes and the verification of identity and difference.

3. The gradual separation or abstraction of that common element from the individuals in the class and its formation in the mind purely as an abstract mental image.

4. The union or synthesis of the several ele-

ments found common to all the individuals in the
class into one whole, making the conception
proper.

It must be apparent that the greater the care
taken in verifying the common elements, and the
greater the number of individuals examined, the
more accurate and complete will be the conception.

The preceding paragraphs may be made clearer
by taking some small cubes of different material
and following up the steps through which you
lead the children in helping them to form a conception of a cube. When you think they have a
fair idea of it, put the cubes out of sight and give
them some clay out of which to mold a cube.
The definition of a concept will then mean much
more to you. After helping them to a mental
picture of a square, give them pencils to draw it,
and what has been said will appear still plainer.
Make a number of similar experiments; you will
probably observe that what you are doing is very
much like " teaching school," but that you have
possibly been overlooking the importance of each
step in the notion-building process. The investigation will show you that some children easily
pick out the more important and characteristic
common—that is, like—elements, while others
note the more superficial and the more variable.
As an illustration, one child will speak of the
sphericity of the apples, while another will mention their color; one will note the rib and venation structure of the leaf, while another will be
absorbed in the outline of the margin. The con-

sequence in the first case is that the fundamental likenesses are discovered and a correct conception easily built up, while in the other the differences are noted and an adequate notion is impossible.

All knowledge-getting, however simple or complex the process, results in conceptions—that is, in general notions. The process is a universalizing process—that is, the mind uses the individual to build the general idea. The meaning of every individual is to be found only in the common— the like—elements of the individuals of the class to which it belongs. That the child should be taught to form conceptions accurately, rapidly, and comprehensively needs then no urging.

Judgment is the process of discovering and verifying the relations of things. It has been called the typical act of knowledge. The two great relations are those of identity and difference. These relations may be of form, size, color, texture, movement, quality, quantity, time, space, part and whole, cause and effect, etc. Every sentence is a formal statement of a judgment. The child says the apple is red. He means that the color agrees with his mental pictures of redness. He says that the knife is sharp, and means that its edge agrees with his notion of sharpness. He says that the dog runs fast, that the house is large, the time is long, the tree is far away, the stove is hot, the iron is heavy, the baby is crying, and ten thousand other things, for similar reasons. It was stated in the last paragraph that the knowledge-getting process is a universalizing process. Look now at

each of the above sentences and see that the subject is an individual object, and that the predicate
—that which tells something about the subject—
is an abstract, universal notion or conception that
had already been built up in the mind and with
which it was familiar. The child simply finds and
puts the individual object in the class where it
belongs—the apple with the red things, the knife
with the sharp things, the dog with the fast run-
ners, the house with the large things, the time
with the long things, the tree with the far-away
things, etc.

There are, then, in every judgment, as in every
sentence, a perception and a conception; the former expressed in the subject and the latter in the
predicate. The former is the individual and the
latter the universal. The judgment affirms their
agreement or disagreement. *Judgment*, then, may
be defined *as finding the universal in the individual.* The accuracy of a judgment depends upon
three things: (1) The accuracy of the perception,
or individual notion; (2) the accuracy of the conception, or general notion; (3) the accuracy of
the comparison upon which the idea of agreement
or disagreement is based. Inaccuracy in any one
of these may result in a wrong judgment. You
see again how interdependent are all the knowledge-getting processes. If now you recall the fact
that every mental picture of an object is made up
of things learned about it, you will see that in
reality each element in it is the result of a judgment. You will also see that every affirmative
judgment you may make about an object gives

you a new element to put into the mental picture of it. What is true of the individual notion is also true of the general notion. Judgment, then, is also involved in all apperception. At first it appears in consciousness as a formal effort at discovering likeness and differences, but afterward it is more or less absorbed in the ready apperception of the attributes of objects. It serves as a means of verifying apperception. Psychologically speaking, the test of a judgment is its harmony with the other related judgments already formed.

In its earlier life the child seems to apprehend likeness and difference intuitively—that is, without any special effort at finding them. As already stated, the likeness thus discovered is usually rather of the superficial or the more attractive than of the fundamental order. It is only as he begins to find the less evident or the essential that formal judgment is called into requisition. Here you will discover the principal difference between the judgment of the child and of the man. A knowledge of essentials and of the more universal elements comes only with experience and education. A child's judgment is confined to narrow limits and to few details. It deals almost exclusively with concrete objects. It is often scarcely more than impulse, but profits and grows wiser by experience. Test your children on their judgment of the lengths of several horizontal lines you draw on the blackboard; the heights of people not standing near together; the colors of ribbons shown them; the likenesses of oranges

13

and lemons, of leaves, of grains, of things very
much unlike as well as very much alike. Not
only will you discover how greatly they differ in
their ability to judge, but also how greatly each
child's judgment will vary in the different classes
of objects presented to him. Find out, if possible, the reason in each case.

Judgment proper endeavors to find the relations between two things, ideas, or objects by direct comparison. This process is sometimes called
implicit reasoning, though judgment is certainly
the better term. It often happens, however, that
the comparison can not be directly made between
two objects of thought, but that it can be made
through the medium of a third. This process is
based on the principle that things that are equal
to or like a certain other thing must be equal to
or like each other. If 3 and 1 equal 4, and 2 and
2 equal 4, then 3 and 1 must equal 2 and 2. If
a stick is one foot in length and a second stick is
also one foot in length, the two sticks must be
equal in length. If each of two pencils is like a
third, they must be like each other. If cats have
retractile claws, and this animal is a cat, it must
have retractile claws. The process is still a process
of finding likenesses, or a process of identification.
It is more complex than judgment, because of the
third or intermediate element used for connecting
the other two.

The *reasoning* process may then be defined as
the *operation of the intellect by which the relations
of certain things are found through the medium of
others.* Every reasoning process stated in a com-

pact way takes the general form of the syllogism in which but three elements, or notions, enter. So, more definitely speaking, *reasoning is simply finding the relation of two ideas through the medium of a third.* Note that there are two notions in a judgment and three in a syllogism. The elements or terms of a judgment are notions; the elements of a syllogism are judgments, each judgment in a syllogism having two terms. The following is the general form of the syllogism:

1. y is x.
2. z is y.
3. $\therefore$ z is x.

The part which y plays is easily seen. It simply serves as a medium by which the relation of x and z is discovered. If investigation shows that 1 is true and also that 2 is true, then 3 follows of necessity. 1 is called the major premise, 2 the minor, and 3 the conclusion; x is called the major term, z the minor, and y the middle. The middle term must be a universal or general notion in at least one of the premises. The major and minor terms must mean the same thing, no more, no less, in each place used. A concrete illustration will help to a clearer understanding of the syllogistic form:

All plants have a circulating fluid called sap.

This object is a plant.

$\therefore$ This object has a circulating fluid called sap.

Make other syllogisms of a similar character and see whether such a process is valid.

The illustration just given is known as a deductive syllogism. *Deduction is the reasoning process which proceeds from a general principle to a particular fact.* Its major premise is always some agreed or some proved principle. An example of the former is found in the following:

A polygon having four equal sides and four right angles is called a square.

This polygon has four equal sides and four right angles.

∴ This polygon is a square.

Induction is the reasoning process which proceeds from individual facts to general principles and laws. Unless the major premise of the deductive syllogism is agreed upon or is a definition, it must be established in some way as a basis for the argument. This is done by the inductive process just defined. The major premise in the first concrete syllogism was established in some such way as this: One plant after another was examined until a large number, including almost every kind and variety, had been tested and each was found to contain a circulating fluid. What was found true of so many and under such a variety of conditions was supposed to be true of all plants, and hence the general statement—

All plants have a circulating fluid.

The conclusion in the inductive process is based upon the general belief in the uniformity of nature. It holds that whatever is true of the representatives of a class under a sufficient number of varying conditions may be accepted as true of all the members of the class, and consequently of the class as a whole. The facts in inductive reasoning are drawn from our experiences.

A child quickly learns to draw general conclusions from his experiences. A hot stove or poker or lamp chimney or teakettle burns him, and he quickly decides that hot things burn. This gives him at once the major premise for the deductive syllogism:

Hot things will burn me.

This stove is hot.

∴. This stove will burn me.

In many cases children generalize and reach conclusions too quickly. Often one single experience will prove sufficient to satisfy them. A child is snapped at by a dog, and he immediately concludes that all dogs will bite or snap at him. He is given bitter medicine in a spoon, and thinks that everything offered him in a spoon is bitter. A little friend of mine calls everybody nice who gives her candy. I have some large friends who do the same thing, however! As soon as the child thus generalizes about a class of objects, he makes the application very promptly to an individual case. My little girl was very shy of a stranger one morning, but when I told her that he was my friend she went to him at once, nestling down in his arms as though she had known him familiarly for years. At another time I picked her up at the head of the stairway and started downstairs with her head pointing below. She sprang up instantly, throwing her arms around my neck, exclaiming, "Papa, you will let me fall!" Though I assured her that her "dear papa would not let her fall," she replied, "Well, papa, that is the *falling way*, anyhow!"

Proof is anything that convinces the mind of a fact or principle. It may come through observation, experimentation, or reasoning. There can be no reliable reasoning which is not based upon accurate and many-sided observation and experimentation. As the mind of the child is satisfied with so little evidence, it is also easily moved to change its views, particularly if pleasure or advantage appears. Henry's mother easily secured a promise from him that he would not play marbles for keeps, but when he saw that he was the best player at school he changed his mind about it. The child's reasoning must be in large measure about concrete things, but the process needs no less careful training on this account. Transition is not made at once to abstract reasoning. That comes gradually. Ability to comprehend the abstract comes only by long practice in comprehending the concrete. Every effort to force the former will prove an injury to the child.

There is a physiological side to reasoning as well as to perception. Brain cells are the machinery by which the mind thinks. They are, like every other part of the body, developed and perfected by intelligent exercise. Brain control comes much in the same way as muscular control. Nerve centers are built up, correlated, and made responsive to the varying and increasingly complex demands of the mind only in Nature's way and in Nature's time. Recent investigations show that the nerve cells of the brain probably grow with mental activity by putting out branches that interlace more or less with each other, building up "apperception masses" that act together under appropriate stimuli, thus indefinitely multiplying the mind's capacity for work. Everybody knows how hard it is to think when his "brain won't work." There is more philosophy in the statement, however, than *everybody* supposes. A brain that is accustomed to light thinking will no more think deeply than will the hands of a pianist accustomed to light and catchy music play at sight the highest creations of the masters. It is as difficult to train the uncultivated brain of an adult to think and to reason out great problems as it is to train the fingers of a full-grown man to become expert at the piano or the violin. If the mind of a Newton were placed in the head of a forester, it would be even more helpless from lack of a proper brain than would the mind and genius of Paderewski from lack of supple fingers if placed in the brain of a blacksmith. The education of the thinking and reasoning activities of the child, then, should not be postponed to the later years of his school life, but should conscientiously and intelligently accompany every stage in his development. When a child, he ought to be permitted to think and to reason as a child. He has plenty of things to think about and to raise questions about if he is exercising his senses as urged in the opening chapter. Stimulate inquiry and investigation, and his vision will be wider and deeper with every rising sun.

The first inquiries of the child are more about

what things are. He soon, however, begins to raise questions about the causes of things. He wishes to know why things are so and so. These questions reveal to you the things about which he is probably able to reason. If you have become familiar with children's ways of seeing things, you will hardly fail to find the way to help them in their reasoning processes. First find out what they know about the class in general. If that, applied to the inquiry, does not give the answer, guide them by experimentation and induction to discover the proper principle. Of course, there should be nothing formal or mechanical about the process. If every little detail were followed, interest would die at once. In ordinary reasoning the full form of the syllogism is seldom thought out even by adults, much less by children. By a single movement the middle term is seen to connect the other two, and their identification is at once announced.

Remember, again, that the end of all knowledge-getting is the building up of general or universal notions, and that, as the object of a judgment is to add another element to the mental image already forming, so the reasoning process, though by a little longer route, serves the same purpose.

CHAPTER XVIII.

THE SELF, HABIT, AND CHARACTER.

THE term *self* has been used frequently in the foregoing pages. It may now be more clearly explained. *By the self is meant the child, the man, as the subject from which conscious phenomena constantly rise.* It is that which responds to the stimuli from the outside world; that which feels and thinks and wills. Its manifold activities constitute what is called mind. The self is distinguished from them only as substance is distinguished from its qualities or attributes. Essentially the self is as its attributes or activities. Knowing them, we know ourselves and other selves also.

In speaking of the various mental activities, there is frequently a suggestion that they are more or less independent parts of the self, and that as one of them is acting the others are at rest. Modern psychologists are agreed, however, that the self acts as a unit in all cases. If apperceiving, it is the whole self that apperceives; if recollecting, it is the whole self that recollects. The interdependence of all the intellectual activities is thus made more evident.

Whatever the self does reacts upon it, giving it

the power to do the same thing again with more ease and more rapidity than before. The more frequently the fingers perform certain movements, the more successfully do they perform each succeeding movement. What is it that is stored up in the fingers as a result of each effort? Nothing but ability to do it again, possibly a little better and with a little less exertion. In the course of time the fingers become organized, as it were, to execute. those particular movements, and their efficiency is thus greatly multiplied. In the same way the reaction of mental activity upon the self is constantly organizing it and increasing its power to act. In this way skill comes, and readiness, and comprehension. In this way also come tendencies and dispositions. Though the child be working objectively, thinking about things outside of himself and making forms and colors to his fancy, *he is really making himself.* It is this that gives a child's environments, a child's companions, a child's books, and a child's plays such tremendous significance in character-building. The nature of mental food and mental exercise affects the nature of the mental organism far more profoundly than the nature of physical food and physical exercise affects the bodily organism. Read Hawthorne's Great Stone Face, and then verify what has been said by a study of the children in your circle.

The study just suggested will possibly reveal some puzzling problems. Apparent contradictions of these statements may be found, but their explanation will usually appear in the hereditary dispositions or in the influences at first overlooked. Read J. G. Holland's *Social Undertow* for further enlightenment.

You have already seen that, as these activities organize into and become a part of the self, they become what is called *habit*. At first they are more or less strange and unfamiliar, more or less difficult of execution. That which makes them familiar and easily executed also makes them a part of the self. Nothing is familiar which has not been converted into terms of the self. Understanding and repetition are the two factors that best bring this about, though the latter often does it in a mechanical way. *Habit is defined as activity resulting from the identification of an action with the self through repetition.* When conditions similar to those originally accompanying an act occur, that act automatically—that is, without conscious effort—tends to repeat itself. This is in accord with the law of physical and mental activity that *when any element of a series recurs, the whole series tends to recur also.* The momentum of habit thus carries an act on to completion, leaving the mind free to give attention to any unfamiliar element present. For illustration, when the child has learned to walk, he moves about the yard looking at the birds and talking about them to his little friends, all the while unconscious of efforts at walking. He is watching the birds and is absorbed in them, and yet he is constantly talking to them or about them, words coming as needed, no effort now being required to recall them or to pronounce them.

All education takes the form of habit. Noth-

ing is valuable as knowledge or skill that is not
so fully possessed and assimilated with the self
that it reacts spontaneously and directly to its appropriate stimulus. Habit makes apperception
possible. Control is attained with habit. It explains the marked differences among men in
their ability to perform certain kinds of work.
Ability is called skill, but it becomes skill only
as it becomes habit. Both mental and physical skill comes from practice that makes it habit. A man's strength or weakness lies in his
habits of thinking and doing. His habits reveal his character, or, better, *his habits are his
character.*

Activities that take the form of habit become
permanent characteristics of the self as well as its
controlling forces. From certain activities come
all that brood of evil habits so common among
people of all ages—laziness, shiftlessness, pro-
crastination, listlessness, slovenliness, skepticism,
faithlessness to promises, lying, instability, fault-
finding, scolding, self-indulgence, etc. Most fortunately also come from others the habits that
make for righteousness—industry, thrift, punctu-
ality, neatness, accuracy, interest, stability, self-
denial, truthfulness, gentleness, courage, etc.
These facts make it possible for the child to realize any ideal of character he may set up. They
also show the part the teacher and parent may
take in the process.

Children easily form and easily break habits.
Their imitative instincts serve them well. It is
usually otherwise with adults. The second part

of the first statement is disputed by many mothers. By sad experience they have learned how
hard it is to break some bad habits into which
their children fall. When, however, they have
secured the co-operation of the children, the work
is less difficult, so the statement is permitted to
stand. It is admitted, though, that there may
be some hopeless cases. A boy, a neighbor of
mine, when but seven years of age gravely con-
fided to his playmate the conclusion that he had
chewed tobacco so long that it would be impossible for him to abstain from it! Another of still
more tender years had formed such a habit of
lying that correctives proved of no avail. Another
fell to fighting nearly every boy he met. Probably every household has its truant and its child
that goes into spasms and turns "black and
blue" whenever punished or denied anything it
craves.

Many of these so-called habits, however, are
superficial, and mere temporary stages in the
growth of the child. A little friendly counsel re-
enforced by wise punishment, if necessary, usually
corrects them. Dr. D. M. Harris, of St. Louis, tells
me that he spent a few hours one afternoon and
a short time on the following morning in showing a little girl how she could talk without stammering. She had stammered so long that it was
supposed to be a physical defect, and efforts at
its cure had been abandoned. Imagine her mother's delight at the dinner table to hear her speak
without any hesitation or defective enunciation
whatever. Children often insist that they can

not overcome certain bad habits that some reminder will readily assist them in correcting. A
friend of mine tells me that a little nephew of
hers would swear like a trooper when angry. He
agreed with his mother that it was very wicked,
but he " got so mad." At the conclusion of a loving talk with him one day about the habit, she
tied a string around one of his fingers and secured
a solemn promise that as long as that string was
there he would not swear. Early in the afternoon of the day after he came rushing into the
house, crying, " Mamma, mamma, cut this string
off my finger quick! " She said, " Why, my
boy? " " Oh," he replied, " I am mad at a boy
out in the alley, and I must swear at him; cut it
quick! "

As has been remarked already, children's
habits, whether good or bad, are easily formed;
hence the danger of indulging them too frequently
in certain cute expressions and willful pranks.
The first " I won't do it! " often provokes a smile,
but too often it is not long before it brings hot,
scalding tears. Study the habits of your children,
and discover the circumstances under which they
have risen. Why do some of them lounge constantly? Why do some walk with a light, elastic
step and others in a shuffling way? Why do some
chew their tongues when they write? Why are
some tidy and neat and others dirty and slovenly?
Why are some always losing things? Why are
some invariably ahead of their fellows and others
as surely behind them? Why are some always
alert and attentive, and others diffident and

listless? Why are some constantly complaining
and grumbling? Why do some always speak
in a loud, self-important way? Why are some
so reserved and shy? Why are some habitually blundering, while others seldom make a
mistake? Why are some frequently breaking
things and others not? Why are some hurting
themselves daily and others seldom meeting a
mishap? Why are some continually asking questions, while others seldom do it? Why do some
usually forget, while others seem to remember
everything they meet? Why are some habitually
open and frank, while others are reticent and reserved? In seeking answers to these questions,
you should not overlook the valuable assistance
each child's family may give you, especially the
father and mother. Remember that the mere discovery that such habits exist will be of little value.
You know that now. Their origin and their correction in each case are the special objects of this
study.

Experiment with the children in habit-break-
ing and habit-forming. Discover the relation of
the understanding and the emotions. Find under
what conditions a child will promptly break a
habit. Is a bad habit more easily displaced by
suppressing it directly or by building up other
habits of an opposite tendency, thus accomplish-
ing it indirectly? What classes of good or bad
habits appear to affect habits in general? What
methods do you find helpful in building up right
habits of thinking and doing? What elements in
the child seem to give him stableness of character?

What effect have children's plays upon their character? Review now the functions of physical, intellectual, prudential, and moral control in the process of character-forming. In what way are they interdependent?

CHAPTER XIX.

CHILDREN'S INSTINCTS AND PLAYS.

Instinct is an inborn disposition to certain activities. It manifests itself in impulses more or less efficiently directed to the attainment of specific ends. The stimulus to action may come from external or internal sources. When the cold " affects the nervous system of the wild goose in a. northern latitude, an impulse to action develops and the bird flies to a warmer clime." When a duck goes into the water, the contact awakens the impulse to paddle. " When certain internal stimuli make themselves felt in the caterpillar, it begins at once to weave its shroud." " Prompted by an internal stimulus, the bird starts to build its nest; the human being to mate, to search for a home, and to take up the round of domestic duties toward which his ancestors were likewise impelled. Blind impulses due to nervous tension have from the beginning of history driven men to do certain things." Such an impulse causes a mother to shield her child, a panic-stricken army to flee, a youth to become an artist, an explorer, a scientist, or a philanthropist. These inherent tendencies or instincts predetermine in large measure the history of each life.

14

The impulse to the satisfaction of the child's first cravings for food suggests at once the idea that all instincts are implanted in the child to satisfy certain general demands of his nature, or, probably better, to impel to the realization of the possibilities of his nature. The impulse to exercise is not purposeless. It develops strength and skill. Both anticipate future needs. The impulse to perception, to know things present to the senses, calls into exercise knowledge-getting activities that later are to grapple with the great problems of the universe. The impulse to imitation serves to stimulate both physical and mental activity, and to make education and progress possible. The impulse to expression devises a multitude of ways and means by which mind may communicate its ideas to other minds and, as a result, it produces all-comprehensive language, the rarest creation of the human intellect.

Out of these impulses and instincts have come science and art and philosophy, with their manifold blessings for the race. But these instincts alone would have left man an isolated, selfish being, finding pleasure only in the gratification of his own personal desires. Wholly absorbed with his own interests, he would have little regard for the interests of others. His fellows would have borne no nearer relation to him than that borne by other objects, animate or inanimate, in the world about him. The instinct that leads him to seek the companionship of his fellows, and that finds satisfaction in their presence, their sympathy, and their co-operation, gives at once a higher meaning to the other instincts mentioned. The end of all this is not simply the happiness and perfection of the individual, but of the race as well. *This impulse to fellowship is called the social instinct.*

Some of the higher species of animals live in pairs, others in communities, flocks, or herds. Man mates, but lives also in communities. The hermit or the recluse is always regarded as an abnormal man. His mode of life interests but seldom attracts. The loneliness of Robinson Crusoe will ever continue to arouse the sympathies of people of all ages. Even in robust health few men or women like to be long alone. When sickness comes, no better medicine than a sympathetic friend can be found. Homesickness is a universal disease. The social instinct draws people together everywhere. It sets them to serving each other. It finds gratification in the happiness and prosperity of all. It recognizes common interests, mutual dependence. It bands the people together for mutual protection. It organizes enterprises for the good of the community as a whole; it establishes schools, churches, governments. The same instinct that draws individuals together into communities draws communities together into larger communities and into states. Thus it awakens the love of home, the love of kindred and of native land. Thus it begets the various institutions of civilization.

The utter helplessness of the newborn babe confirms, if confirmation were necessary, the idea that man was intended to be a social being. Next

to its physical demands come the demands for
the presence of another person. With each first
waking moment how imperatively is this demand
expressed! With what satisfaction does the child
nestle in the warm bosom of its mother and with
what manifestations of delight does it soon welcome the coming of the different members of the
household! Few observers have failed to note the
intense interest with which children meeting for
the first time contemplate one another and how
short an association may make them necessary to
each other's happiness. Millions of children have
been shut in or tied up because they persisted in
running away to the home of a neighbor in order
to find some one of their own age to engage in
play. The most interesting thing to a little boy
or girl is another little boy or girl, hobbyhorses
and dolls not excepted. To the child who has
had the pleasure of playing with another child
there is nothing else in the way of amusement
quite so desirable. In many ways older people
satisfy this longing of the child for fellowship,
but the sweetest joys of childhood are missed by
the child that has no playmates of approximately
his own age.

A study of the plays of children shows their
great resemblance to the more serious occupations
of their elders. Children plan and execute with
an interest and an energy that flag only when the
weary little body demands rest and sleep. They
strive to imitate almost every conceivable thing
that their elders do. They build houses, make
mud pies, plant corn, go to town, teach school,

give parties, play doctor, dress the dolls, wash
clothes, build fires, break colts, hold revival serv-
ices, run lemonade stands, give circus perform-
ances, play soldier, hive the bees, make garden,
dig coal mines, write letters, banter, quarrel, fight,
kill! The earnestness with which they do all
this shows its intense reality to them, and shows
further that the instincts of childhood do not differ greatly from the instincts of manhood. Play
foreshadows the occupations soon to follow. In
it the imitative, the inventive, the expressive, the
social instincts of the child find their normal satisfaction. Play thus becomes the first great period
of apprenticeship in the life of the child. In it
that physical and intellectual control is attained
which assures easy transition to skill in doing
work. Play as well as other activities reacts upon
the child and helps to make him what he is.

How, then, can any one overlook the importance of the child's plays? How can any parent
or teacher fail to take an abiding interest in everything that the child attempts to do? The character of his play needs the same attention as that
given to the character of his food. Some plays
call the imitative activities into exercise more
prominently than others, some the inventive, some
the apperceptive. Some plays quicken the judgment, others the memory; some call out the reasoning powers, others the imaginative; some develop muscular strength, others skill. Some children engage in the same play all day long, others
require frequent change; some prefer quiet plays,
others the noisy and boisterous; some insist

on playing indoors, others seek the free open air; some incline to plays that symbolize industrial occupations, others to those that symbolize nature or adventure; some choose games or plays in which there is a contest of mind, others those in which the contest is one of physical strength or skill. A recent inquiry among a large number of boys of eight years of age and upward shows that the popular games among them are black man, crack the whip, duck on the rock, boxing, baseball, football, etc. The reason almost invariably given was that " it is such fun to beat somebody! " In some cases the brutal nature crept out a little too clearly, for such expressions as the following were not uncommon: " It is such sport to see a fellow tumble over and hurt himself! " " Sometimes you can knock a fellow and black his eye." " It is so funny to see the boys and girls fly off the whip and then go limping away! " " Because you can break an arm or leg sometimes." " If you watch, you can knock the breath out of him." Test the children on all these points. Discover whether the boys and girls like to play together and the reasons for it. What do all these different preferences indicate? What effect have certain classes of plays had upon the school work of the children?

The range of a child's plays should be so wide and so carefully selected as to be developing every side of his nature. The kindergarten is most happily organized for this purpose; a study of its principles and methods will throw much light upon the problem. The kindergarten, however, is

a school, even though its whole aim is to direct
the play instinct of the child, and therefore fails
in retaining fully the most essential elements in all
true play—spontaneity and freedom. The range is
also necessarily very limited. It presupposes a
wide range of home plays, and makes them contribute to its own games and plays. In fact, it
strives to correlate them all in such a way as to
make them mutually helpful. The investigation
suggested in the last paragraph will show that in
nearly every community there are many children
who not only have a very limited range of plays,
but who are also ignorant of the fact that there
are any other plays than those with which they
are acquainted. They are narrowed and dwarfed
and starved from lack of wholesome, stimulating,
thought-provoking plays. When they enter school
or start to learn some trade the effect of it all is
evident enough.

What the children play is no more momentous
than how they play. Useful plays may be de-
vised in abundance, and yet unsatisfactory results
follow. The liberal hand is not always the wise
hand. To attain the highest good, plays should
succeed each other in the order best adapted to
the child's capacities and needs. A child may en-
tertain himself day after day for a year with the
same play, but there can be little growth in it for
him after a few successive repetitions. Of course,
the child's pleasure must be consulted in the se-
lections, else his plays will be of little profit to
him. It usually requires very little tact to control his choice, though there is always danger of

a mother following her own notions and convenience rather than the needs of the child. ⟨It is
always safer to find out the child's instincts and
be governed by them.⟩ The philosophy of a play
is a very profound thing on the mother's side
and a very exacting thing on the child's side.
In nothing else may superficial child study so
easily reveal itself as in the management of play.
Children should be taught how to play with
the same care that they are taught later in life
how to work. If properly led and instructed, they
learn a thousand things in their plays that become a valuable and a permanent part of their
mental and physical being. Many girls become
good seamstresses in cutting and fitting dolls'
dresses. Many boys learn how to use simple tools
in playing carpenter. A little friend of mine
learned more about silkworms by caring for a
few eggs given her and watching the hatching and
the metamorphoses through the spinning of the
cocoons and the flight of the moths than nine
tenths of the high-school students get out of books
on entomology. Another became a fair artist in
playing with his pencils and his water-color
paints. Another learned many interesting facts
about great writers in playing "authors," and in
after years at school succeeded in passing an examination in which that knowledge served her
well. Are not many of Whitcomb Riley's poems
surcharged with images garnered in childhood's
plays and wanderings? The vividness with which
Shakespeare describes "the dainty, dew-impearled
flowers, the shadowy forests and the wide-skirted

meads, the weaving spiders and the honey-bags of the bumblebees, the banks where the wild thyme blows and the nodding violet grows," tells plainly enough how he romped and played on many a knoll up and down the beautiful valley of the quiet Avon. It also discloses how richly these ramblings endowed him for the great work of his mature life.

The effect of play upon the social life of the child and upon his character depends much upon its management. If two children play together happily, one must deny himself all the time for the pleasure of the other, or they must make mutual concessions. Few small children are known to play together for any great length of time without quarreling. One of them may yield to the other for awhile, but selfishness overreaches itself at last and rebellion results. The issue must be settled by an appeal to arms or by concessions from the aggressor. A few lessons usually suffice to convince children that the latter is the better way. Members of the household, particularly the parents, may aid the process greatly by discreet observation, wise repression, and sympathetic counsel. The child is naturally a despot. He knows that he is to rule, and often thinks that he is to rule others rather than himself. His plays furnish the opportunity for the simple lessons in democracy which he needs in order to anticipate the more responsible duties of neighbor and citizen.

CHAPTER XX.

The social instinct, along with all other human instincts, is inventive. It is not satisfied merely with the presence of other people. It soon begins to devise ways and means for its completer gratification. It profits by experiences, as already explained, and learns to respect the individuality of others. It takes pleasure in their pleasure. It grieves when they suffer. It identifies itself with them. Sympathy and love, self-denial and service follow. This development being more or less reciprocal in the individual cases, additional ways and means of showing deference and of contributing to the comfort and happiness of one another are easily found. Even children quickly discover that which will please others, and often with rare generosity seek to bestow it. The principle is not disproved in saying that many children and adults serve others because they expect a service in return, nor in saying that they labor to make other people happy because their sensitiveness to the condition of others is so great that they are miserable on seeing them unhappy.

Out of this spirit of companionship and good will have risen the code of manners generally observed in good society. Even Bushmen and Patagonians observe simple forms of etiquette in their social intercourse. Pirates and outlaws are as exacting in certain social requirements as are the Knickerbockers of New York city. The simple folk of the Scotch Highlands and the humble peasantry of the Tyrol are models of courtesy and good breeding. All civilized people are governed by social customs that are held in as high esteem as the statute laws. They touch every phase of the domestic and the community life. They include the relation of master and servant, of superior and inferior, of peers and equals, of old and young, of friends and strangers, of the same sex and of opposite sexes; they include the proprieties of the street, the railway car, the church, the club, the public assembly, the parlor, the dining room, etc. Few men who are lacking in good manners are successful in business or professional life. The secret of the art of managing men is found largely in the art of treating them courteously. Emerson says that "address, good manners, rules the world." It makes friends, it wins votes, it brings trade, it opens the door to the social circle, it forwards diplomacy, it disarms hostility, it secures co-operation, it everywhere contributes to the comfort and the enjoyment of mankind. The utility of good manners is often overlooked in the education of children.

Mere politeness should not be confused with good manners. The former is simply the observance of external forms. The latter is the generous expression of the self in friendly deference to others. Politeness is more or less studied and artificial; good manners are sympathetic and spontaneous. The former is put on as occasion demands, the latter are so fully a part of the self that they are never easily cast aside. Affectation tries to hide itself in politeness; sincerity expresses itself in good manners. All efforts to teach the children the forms of social intercourse without exalting the kindly spirit above the graceful act must result in making them merely polite. A selfish child may be polite, but not good-mannered. The essential in all cases is a large heart, a warm heart, and an honest heart. Good manners are bred into children; politeness is put on the outside of them. To know how to act in company is but a small part of good manners; it is just as important to know how to act in the family circle and in the associations of everyday life.

The development of good manners in children is largely dependent upon the presence of good manners in the home. If affection and personal solicitude for each other's comfort control the actions of the older people that gather round the hearthstone, the little children will hardly be long in catching the spirit as well as the action. Children reared in such homes are usually easy and self-possessed in any company. They are not obliged to " put on " when among strangers, and consequently they suffer little embarrassment at any time.

As previously suggested, every child needs friendly counsel and advice concerning his actions toward others. There may be occasions

when he needs to be reminded that he is petulant
or selfish, angry or boisterous, forward or obtrusive,
thoughtless or cruel, uncouth or vulgar, imperti-
nent or disrespectful. There certainly are occasions
when he needs to be shown how to be gentle and
considerate, to control his temper and to respect
the rights of others, to be self-sacrificing and generous, to be modest and retiring. These virtues
lie at the very basis of good manners. Every
child is entitled to be taught also the simple matters of form in table etiquette, in entering and
leaving the homes of others, in meeting people
in the street, in inviting or accepting the company of others, in welcoming and entertaining
guests, etc. It is difficult to separate good manners from grace of body and from grace in sitting, standing, walking, talking, and gesture.
These make up part of the social as well as the
physical education of the child.

In the study of the social life of children the
inquiries, as in other investigations suggested,
should embrace both the facts and their causes.
Why are some children coarse and ill-mannered,
while others from the same home are refined and
agreeable? Why are some familiar with the
forms of polite society, and yet arrogant and boor-
ish in their relations to other children? Why are
some children great favorites with their classmates, while others have few friends? Why are
some naturally affable and popular, while others
are disagreeable in spite of every effort to please?
How closely allied to good manners are habits of
cleanliness and neatness, good morals, etc.?

Manners and morals are not separated very far from each other. Rosenkranz says that moral culture is the essence of social culture. As explained in the preceding paragraphs, all social forms have had their origin in the desire to multiply and enhance the pleasures of social intercourse. That desire rises from love and sympathy, the crowning graces of the ideal moral and religious life. Prudential action—that is, action for advantage or profit to the self—may be characteristic of much business and social intercourse. If, however, the action is prompted by the motive of good to others, it becomes moral. Prudential control suggests the idea of *getting;* moral control, the idea of *being.* The test of a man's prudence is in what he *has;* of his morals, in what he *is.* The distinguishing characteristics of the former are foresight, vigilance, industry, economy, courage, self-possession, perseverance, self-interest; of the latter, integrity, sincerity, fidelity, forbearance, sympathy, gentleness, temperance, meekness, purity, brotherly kindness, charity. Prudential control raises the question, *What profit?* Moral control, *What good?* In prudential control the motive is always advantage; in moral control, it may be the good or the bad. The former is judged by its attainments; the latter by its motives.

The moral idea grows out of the social. The latter recognizes the relations of individuals to each other. The former recognizes its obligation to realize those relations. Whatever it can do to benefit others becomes duty; whatever it can do for the self which will enhance its power to serve others is also duty. It builds up a personal ideal whose realization becomes a duty, a consuming desire. Actions in conformity with it are called right; those in opposition are called wrong. It is readily seen that moral emotions, moral affections, and moral desires develop with moral ideas. Moral control is attained in the same general way as physical, intellectual, and prudential control, and is the end of all the others. Herbart says that that education which has not morality for its supreme end must result in hopeless confusion.

The child's impulses are to be true. Temptation to be untrue comes when he wishes to shield himself against ridicule or punishment, or to astonish somebody by a big story. Every one has noticed how particular a little child is to have the minutest details of an incident correctly given. If mother, in relating some household incident that occurred the day before, happens to omit a part of it which she does not care to repeat to the visitor, little Mary is sure to remind her of it and to tell it herself. Erroneous or incomplete notions of a thing at the time of its occurrence easily explain the tenacity with which children cling to wrong statements they afterward make concerning it. In other cases, faulty memory, laziness, or indifference may explain what appears to be a deliberate falsehood. Whatever the cause of misrepresentation, the tendency soon becomes a habit unless promptly checked. Once a habit, it begins to breed every sort of deception, and to corrupt the whole moral nature of the child.

Truth and sincerity are the basic virtues in all morality. Without them there can be no moral character.

Only when a child begins to distinguish between right and wrong may he be said to have a moral character. The moral element begins to appear when he does what his parents tell him to do because he loves and respects them; when for the same reason he denies himself the pleasure of gratifying a desire to do a forbidden thing. It certainly is not present when he obeys them from fear of punishment—a cat or a dog does the same thing. I once heard a little girl say to her mother, " I did not read that book, because I thought you would not wish me to do it." That is a step further in advance, but she has made greater progress when the discovery that the book is evil immediately begets aversion to it bcause her nature finds no pleasure in it.

Ask a dozen children why they do certain things which you consider morally good, and carefully note their answers. It will not take long to discover that the moral element lies not in the act itself, but in the motive, the intention. Discover the causes which prompted the reasons given by the children. Some will cite the authority of parent or teacher and others will give their own reasons for their answers. Some will probably quote apt maxims and others maxims that have no bearing whatever on the subject. How prominent is the personal or selfish element in the answers?

The moral instinct or impulse of the child

strengthens with every effort he makes to know and to do what is right. The law of reaction is even more clear here than elsewhere. Apperception of the right in each individual case is dependent upon the moral character as then organized; the momentum of the impulse to its realization is similarly dependent. In the beginning he may be doing right things impulsively, or out of pure sympathy, or from a desire to please others, or in obedience to authority, or for personal advantage that may come. Along with the pleasure in right doing gradually develops the sense of obligation and of individual responsibility.

Little progress in moral culture will be making unless the child's ideas of right being and right doing are daily growing more definite and more clear. He must not only love the truth, but must know what is truth; not only desire to be honest, but must be able to discern what is honest; not only love noble conduct, but have the power to recognize it when he sees it; not only hold purity in high esteem, but know in what purity consists; not only love his fellows, but also understand his duties toward them. Many people are negatively good, but lack nearly every active moral virtue.

Conscience is the complex activity which discerns right and wrong and impels to right action. Its simple analysis shows—

1. A general idea or conception of right.

2. Judgment as to the conformity of a particular act to the general idea.

15

3. A feeling of obligation to do what the judgment affirms to be right.

4. The effort to perform the act.

5. The feeling of satisfaction accompanying and following the effort, or dissatisfaction if no effort is made.

With this analysis before us it is not difficult to see more fully the dependence of moral character upon environment and education. The problems of right action are incomparably higher than any problems of the physical universe. Their solution in each individual case requires the co-operation of all the activities of the self. How important, then, that everything entering into the life of the child should be tested by its effect upon his moral nature!

The reason for urging a clear understanding of the real nature of good manners now hardly needs an explanation. If the nobleness of spirit has been keeping pace with the nobleness of manners, the transition to good morals is already made. If otherwise, the child has simply been given the power to cover up his true nature and to deceive his fellows at his will.

The presentation and development of right motives in children is the most delicate problem in education. The exercise of authority or of force will not accomplish it. Nagging and scolding make little progress toward it. Rewards and prizes will not do much better. Advantage and profit unduly exalt self-interest. Words of appreciation and of praise may stimulate to right doing. Respect and affection for others may serve as a powerful restraint against evil. Some of these will have but a temporary effect in promoting right conduct, while all will lack the essence of the moral life—*the impulse to do right for right's sake alone, regardless of personal pleasure, personal profit, or of profit to others.*

This statement should not be construed as meaning that the motives named are at all times unwise and hurtful. All of them, not even excepting the second, may profitably be used in the different stages of the child's development. There are times when he is incapable of appreciating any other motive than that of physical force. There are other times when he will more quickly respond to a promised reward, or to suggestions of advantage, or to words of encouragement, or to an appeal from one whom he respects and loves, or to the simple assurance that an act in question is right. In the development of the child's motives, the following simple rules will be found valuable:

1. Use negative or restrictive motives sparingly, relying rather upon positive motives or incentives.

2. Appeal to the motive which the child can appreciate.

3. Appeal constantly to the highest motive the child can appreciate.

4. Improve each vantage gained to educate the child to appreciate a higher motive.

5. Eliminate the personal or selfish element as rapidly as possible.

6. Be patient for results. Relax vigilance only

when the impulse to the good dominates the child's entire being.

Make the question of motives a frequent study in the management of your children. At what age, if any, are they disposed to ignore the authority of their superiors? In what way, if any, does the pubescent period affect the manners and morals of children? What effect has home training had upon them? Are you ruling some of them by sheer authority or by brute force? Are you satisfied simply with their co-operation, even though secured by a low motive, or are you using the various means at your command for developing higher ideals for right action? Are you appreciating the sensitiveness of some of the rare little souls intrusted to your care and are you giving them that sympathy and counsel for which they crave every hour of the day? Are you on the alert for the slightest indication of a better spirit and a readier service in each child? Are you living so blameless that every time the child's life touches yours he is quickened to nobler endeavor?

CHAPTER XXI.

NORMAL means natural or conformable to a type. The term may be applied to a child that at birth has a perfect body or to one whose physical or mental development is approximately the same as that of the average child of an equal age. If imperfectly formed, or if much beyond or behind in development, he is called abnormal. The term abnormal may be applied to a child who is unusually bright for his age as well as to one who is unusually stupid; to one who is excessively large for his age as well as to one who is particularly small. It is also applied to any one who is misshapen in any way, or who has unnatural enlargement or atrophy of any physical organ. The variation should be sufficiently marked to be readily noticeable in each case before the term abnormal can be properly applied.

Unusually bright children are often called precocious; unusually dull, defective. The term exceptional is applied to both classes by many writers. The child of six years of age that knows as much as the average child of ten is as much an object of interest and inquiry as the child at ten that knows no more than the average child at

179

six. There is scarcely a schoolroom anywhere in which both are not found. Some children have fine memories, and yet seem utterly wanting in judgment; others remember practically everything they hear, but can recall little that they see. Occasionally a child is met that has prodigious mathematical ability and yet can not be made to understand the merest rudiments of language or of science.

Many children seem to be perfectly formed externally, and yet are seriously defective in one or more of the special senses or in some of the vital organs. While the per cent of children seriously defective at birth is small, the per cent more or less deficient is much larger than many people suppose. Occasionally a family is found in which every child is defective physically, the defect being of the eye in one, of the ear in another, possibly of both in a third, of motor control in a fourth, a defect of the brain or of some other organ in a fifth. In many families but one defective child may be found, the others being perfectly formed. In some families a child with a serious physical blemish has not been known for generations.

Some physically deformed children seem to be little more than freaks, so subtle are the causes producing the deformities. Several cases coming within my personal knowledge are so unusual on both sides of the family that the recognized laws of heredity do not account for them. In some cases the failure of certain bones to ossify properly, the arrested development of the cerebral tissues, the paralysis of the motor nervous system, the withering or shrinking of an arm or a leg, the atrophy of a special sense, seems to be due to some adventitious or accidental cause, as is frequently seen in other animals and in plants. In many children the physical deformities are easily traceable to measles, mumps, spotted fever, spinal meningitis, typhoid fever, whooping-cough, scarlet fever, scrofula, smallpox, and other diseases. In such cases, the physical deformity is not usually accompanied by an impairment of the mental faculties. Investigations show that in a large majority of cases spinal curvature, bandy legs, pigeon toes, and distortions of similar character are due to bad habits in sitting, standing, or walking in childhood. Not a few of them may be charged to the unsatisfactory desks in use in the schools. Inherited weakness may be the remote cause in many cases, but proper care might have prevented serious perversion.

Inherited diseases and deformities may be traced to one of three general causes: a similar disease or deformity in one or both parents, constitutional weakness in one or both, or bad habits in one or both. Instances without number might be cited to prove the regularity with which the law of heredity transmits the infirmities of the parents to the children. Its significance would be most appalling were it not for the fact that the same law governs the transmission of physical excellence, and that wise treatment may largely overcome the evils of heredity. Parents conscious of their own constitutional tendencies have by a rigid system of hygiene maintained such a vigorous physical tone in themselves and in their children that the prospective affections have been entirely averted. The presence of any constitutional or chronic malady in either parent is always evidence of its probable appearance in the children, and if this study does nothing more than put those in authority over them on the alert for the discovery and for the intelligent treatment of such cases, it will deserve well of mankind. It is an interesting fact that certain apparently opposite physical temperaments, though constitutionally weak, bring forth strong and healthy offspring. This tendency to mutual correction shows itself even in trivial irregularities. A neighbor's nose pointed distinctly to the right. The nose of his wife pointed to the left. The daughter's nose was normal!

The effect of the habits and occupations of the parents upon their children needs special emphasis. A few generations of musicians insure the fingers of the coming children to be well adapted to play upon musical instruments. The children of the lacemakers inherit that delicacy and suppleness of the muscles of the hand by which their ancestors have ever excelled their competitors in the markets of the world. Insurance companies not only lay great stress upon the constitutional tendencies of a candidate's ancestors, but also upon his personal habits as well. Anything that affects a man's vitality affects that of his future offspring also. The long train of physical infirmities in children that may easily be traced to narcotic habits in one or both parents is well known. The responsibility that a persistent user of alcohol or tobacco assumes is now so clearly established that it seems superfluous to appeal to statistics concerning it.

In the matter of eyesight alone, Dr. T. H. Dinsmore discovers thirty-one defectives out of eighty-six children whose fathers were addicted to alcoholic beverages. Out of three hundred and ninety-nine children whose fathers used tobacco before and after marriage, two hundred and twenty-four had weak eyes. The inquiries included children of old soldiers who used tobacco before their children were born, and it was found that one hundred and ten out of one hundred and fifty-six examined had impaired vision. It is conceded that some of the responsibility should be attributed to the hardships of the field, and possibly to other causes, but the summary contains a plain warning. One of Dugdale's Juke tables shows that but one out of nineteen temperate Jukes was diseased, and that ten out of thirteen intemperate were in ill health. Dr. Tatham, the British registrar-general, believes that the use of alcohol is the chief cause of excessive death rates, and says that the liquor trades are fatal to those who engage in them. His figures show the clergy to be the healthiest people in the world.

In Physical degeneration in parents, whether caused by alcoholism, the opium habit, licentiousness, or excesses of any other kind, seldom fails to manifest itself in some way in the bodies of its progeny. Sometimes the subtle poison does not begin its work until manhood or middle life, but it often discloses its presence in the cradle. Nervous disorders, scrofulous tendencies, proneness to epilepsy, pulmonic weakness, and kindred affections, with their mournful train of miseries, tell too plainly that somebody has violated the laws of Nature. Joseph Cook quotes Oliver Wendell Holmes as saying, in response to the declaration that any disease may be cured if a physician is called early enough, that the statement is true, "but 'early enough' would usually mean two hundred years in advance." Miss Clark, a high authority, says: "The imbecile is the result of corrupt living, frequently of guilt, sometimes of a line of ancestry unbrightened for a generation by a single responsible moral individual. In every case where a child has not been made imbecile through some prenatal shock, accident, or sickness, somewhere in the family annals there have been opium eating, immoral living, drunkenness, insanity, imbecility, or actual crime—perhaps all." Thirty-four per cent of the imbecile children are the immediate offspring of intemperate parents.

Inherited physical deformity means mental deformity, particularly when the former is an affection of the cerebral or sensory nerves, or even of the motor organism. So positively has this been demonstrated that in the treatment of feeble-minded and insane children, as well as of adults, physicians attempt to correct physical disorder first. With the normal physical functions restored, mental equilibrium also ordinarily returns.

Maudsley says, " No one nowadays who is engaged in the treatment of mental disease doubts that he has to do with the disordered function of a bodily organ—of the brain." Ufer asserts that " by far the larger part of mental disturbance in children is due to bodily complaints; a good proportion of these can be cured, whereas, if ignored, incurable diseases will arise."

The gradations from the strictly normal mind to the completely unbalanced mind follow very closely the gradations from the perfect nervous organism to that state of the brain in which all cerebral action is uncontrolled and uncontrollable. Intellectually speaking, the term normal is usually applied to a variety of minds even slightly defective in some directions, just as the term normal is applied to bodies which are approximately perfect. It should be borne in mind that every case varying from the normal, inside and outside the range just named, is, if not merely slow in development, just so much away toward imbecility or insanity. The causes leading to mental defects are, in general, the same as those already mentioned as leading to physical defects. Some investigators think that mental traits are often directly transmitted by inheritance, though others maintain that the physical traits are responsible for the transmission in all cases. However that may be, mental activity and mental growth are dependent upon the facility and exactness with which the physical organism performs its functions. If any of the sense organs be defective, there must be a corresponding lack of perception of the external world, and a consequent retardation in mental development. Superintendent Klock, after a thorough examination of the pupils in the Helena city schools, says that "in cases where children have attended school regularly for from eight to twelve years, and are from six months to two years behind in their grades, the loss of time is due almost invariably to defective eyesight or hearing, one or both." The mind is dependent upon the senses for the material which it elaborates into knowledge. Its higher activities develop normally only as the lower supply material in abundance and variety, hence the disadvantage under which every sense-defective labors.

Physical and mental defectives are, generally speaking, moral defectives. It is well to remember here that a moral defective is not necessarily actively bad. He may be simply motiveless, or without impulse to moral action of any kind. Four classes of morally defective children may be recognized:

1. The harmless, passive sort, little energy, little strength in desire of any kind.

2. Those inclined to the good, though with little will power, easily misled.

3. The stubborn, evil-minded, cruel, sensuous passions prominent, intellectually dull.

4. The cunning, dishonest, inclined to petty thieving and to sneaking tricks, intellectually bright.

All these classes of moral abnormals, more or less defined, are often found in one schoolroom. In a few localities they embrace a dangerously large proportion of the school children. As a consequence their management becomes a most perplexing problem. The intelligent treatment of moral defects must ever depend upon a knowledge of their origin.

Pathologists and criminologists generally agree that the law of heredity accounts for moral temperaments as fully as for the physical and intellectual. The authenticated story of the Juke family already mentioned may be approximately duplicated a thousand times over. In one hundred and fifty years " the descendants of one man, a hunter and fisher, a hard drinker, jolly and companionable, averse to steady toil, working hard by spurts and idling by turns, becoming blind in his old age, and entailing his blindness upon his children and grandchildren," contributed one hundred and forty criminals and offenders, including seven murderers. This showing does not include the long list of paupers, harlots, roustabouts, drunkards, petty thieves undetected, liars, cheats, disturbers of the peace, etc. Ribot tells of an educated man who secretly indulged in the alcoholic habit. Only one of his five children lived to maturity. That one was cruel almost from birth, and delighted in torturing animals in every conceivable way. He soon proved physically and mentally feeble, and at nineteen went to the insane asylum. Morel examined one hundred and fifty " children of the commune." ranging from ten to seventeen years of age, and says: " I am confirmed in my previous convictions as to the baneful effects produced by alcohol, not only in the individuals who use this detestable drink to excess, but also in their descendants. On their depraved physiognomy is impressed the threefold stamp of physical, intellectual, and moral degeneracy."

The transmission of certain kinds of immoral instincts is also clearly established. In some families it is lying; in others, cattle-stealing, homicide, burglary, pocket-picking, quarreling, incendiarism, dishonesty, forgery, licentiousness, etc. Recently a newspaper stated that a noted cattle thief had been killed, and added significantly that several other members of his family are now serving sentences in the penitentiary for cattle-stealing.

But heredity is not the only force effectively at work in a child's early life corrupting his moral nature. Environment, as a deadly nightshade, insidiously pours its venom into his heart. Breathing the fetid air of an ill-ventilated, drunken home, hearing nothing but oaths and obscene words from dissolute and vicious parents, mingling with foul-mouthed, mischief-plotting companions, taught that to lie and steal and fight make the ideal man, is it a wonder that the boy enters school " morally abnormal " ? His hereditary tendency being enforced by such environment and training, it were a miracle if it were otherwise. From such a home as that all the way up to the ideal fireside are homes lacking in varying degrees the spirit and assistance necessary to build up true moral character. Put a child blest with a royal inheritance in such an environment, and what must be his fate?

This much space has been given to illustrate the causes that produce weak and abnormal children in the hope that sufficient interest may be aroused to insure a more exhaustive study of the unfortunates who ever appeal to us for sympathy and help. The average teacher and parent is too much disposed to ignore the presence of these fundamental defects in his children, and to treat them with a harshness that aggravates rather than relieves the infirmity. They overlook the law that the slightly abnormal tendencies of early childhood, unless intelligently corrected, may even in early manhood bring utter ruin to body and mind. *Two seemingly parallel straight lines may be but an inch apart at their origin and yet be ten feet apart at the end of a mile!* Sufficient has been said to show that defectives are common enough to require that all persons intrusted with the care and culture of children should familiarize themselves with the peculiarities of each child's physical, mental, and moral nature, and treat it as its individual needs demand. The average child has been given too much attention; the exceptionals, both above and below the average, too little. There has been a vast waste in our attempts to teach children in the mass rather than as individuals; to force them to come up to certain ideal standards rather than to take the time to find and to apply the means which their individual natures demand. Ignorance and thoughtlessness on the part of parents and teachers will not be excused much longer.

Many teachers accidentally discover facts concerning their pupils after they have done them great injustice. A personal friend tells me that one day a pupil asked for the repetition of an explanation of a principle which he had just given. He had taken much time and great care in giving it and thought all understood it. With conscious impatience, he exclaimed, " I should think that even an idiot could understand that." Her eyes filled with tears and, as the class filed out, she remained in her chair sobbing convulsively. He apologized for his language, and asked why she was so deeply affected. She replied: " Sir, my mother is in an insane asylum, and we children are in constant dread lest we may go there too. I feared you might be telling the truth, and that I am possibly already an idiot." Though he has taught many years since, he assures me that he has never again spoken unkindly to a pupil.

Some years ago a teacher in one of the grades was annoyed by the slowness of one of his pupils, and in desperation took her by the back of the neck and shook her severely. She had been afflicted a long time with spinal weakness, but at the opening of the year her parents hoped her sufficiently convalescent to enter school again. Her slowness was caused by her malady and her intense desire not to do anything which might cause its return. No wonder that was an anxious night in that household! In a spelling class the other day I asked the students to criticise the work of their classmates, and to mark the misspelled words. One of them complained to me that her critic had marked three words in her writing speller that were correctly spelled, *though they had been spelled aloud for her guidance.* The next day I took occasion to speak of the matter, assuring them that each critic would be held responsible for his work. As the class was dismissed, the critic mentioned came to me and confessed. I asked why she did it. She replied: "My eyes! I suppose it must be my eyes." Examination showed that she was right, and her many blunders were all explained. I had occasion once to reprimand, for the third or fourth time, a young woman who had been giving me much anxiety by her repeated indiscretions. She smiled as I spoke of her offenses, and giggled as I assured her that she was at the point of suspension. In surprise, I asked why she received my reproof with such levity. She answered that often when she wanted to cry she laughed, and that often when she wanted to laugh she cried. With a word or two, I excused her from the room and sought further light. It came from a friend, who said: " That young woman has suffered from childhood with epilepsy. For a year or more she had been so nearly well that her parents were assured last summer by her physician that if she could be sent among strangers for awhile she would probably forget her affliction, and in her new surroundings attain perfect health and self-control. She undoubtedly told you the truth about her crying and laughing muscles becoming crossed at times. Epileptics can hardly be expected to be either intellectually or morally normal."

16

A little fellow who was trying "awfully hard" to be good said to his teacher one day: "It is easy for you to be good. Your father was a minister. My father was bad, and drank and swore and gambled, and sometimes I feel that I *must* do just as he did." A young colored girl in the South said to a noble woman who had befriended her, "When I see how wicked so many of my kindred are, I often wonder whether it can be possible that I shall always live an upright life." These children, and thousands of others like them, are in the schools of every State in the Union. And yet you often hear people speak of "the sickly, sentimental doctrine of heredity!"

But in addition to these there is also a great army of children more or less belated in development along some of the lines heretofore mentioned. The bright, active child is encouraged and given a better chance than his sluggish brother. The natural modesty of one and the frowardness of another may explain the difference in their mental growth, for one has hesitated to improve an opportunity without encouragement, while the other boldly took advantage of it. The former fails to get the experience he needs, while the latter may gain even more than he needs. One child is sent to school because he likes to go, and another is kept at home occasionally because he likes work better than school. Ere long he loses class standing and, after a few spasmodic efforts at attendance, drops out of school forever. This whole chapter is a special plea for the children that for the various reasons cited do not get so good a start as some of their more fortunate brothers and sisters. Some of them are the rarest spirits that ever breathed, but all, no matter what their ancestry or what their talents, are entitled to that sympathy and encouragement which will give them an equal chance with their fellows in the struggle for life. The abnormal tendencies of the race are to be corrected by purifying the blood and perfecting the powers of the individual child.

The suggestions already offered in the various chapters will guide in many of these inquiries, but a few additional ones are here given: Note the peculiarities in each child and seek for their causes. If a child is disposed to be active, does his activity have a purpose, or is it evidently aimless and purposeless? Discover whether he is sensitive or hysterical; whether he "goes to pieces" easily; whether he is exceedingly voluble, but apparently knows little about anything; whether, though apparently trying, he is failing to make any progress in the work assigned him; whether he is wanting in ideals and motives; whether he is interested in trivial things or in matters of importance; whether the shape of his head is suggestive of feeble cranial capacity; whether the face indicates unusual cunning or shrewdness; whether the mouth and lips provoke a suspicion of vulgarity or sensuality; whether he is retiring, sullen, despondent, sanguine, persevering, standing still, or growing; whether he is defective in speech or muscular control. Whether he is conscious of his defects and whether his fellow-pupils are treating him in such a way as to increase his embarrassment.

The question frequently arises as to the amount of time that should be given to defective or delinquent children. The answer must be found in the needs of all. The interests of all should not be sacrificed for the benefit of the few. The aggressive, ambitious children must not be held back until the slow ones catch up. Absolute uniformity is impossible, much less desirable. If reasonable time and effort fail to accomplish anything with a child, he should be put exclusively under individual supervision or sent to a school devoted to serious and obstinate defectives. It should not be supposed that child study means the neglect of Nature's favored ones. It means such an acquaintance with every child as will enable the parent and teacher to adopt such methods of instruction and to produce such environments as will insure the most rapid progress possible in the development of all classes.

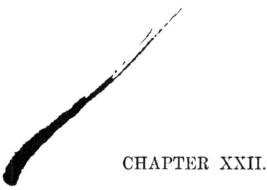

CHAPTER XXII.

STAGES OF GROWTH, FATIGUE POINT, ETC.

For lack of space several important subjects intimately related to the child's growth and well-being must be treated with great brevity.

Infancy, childhood, and youth are the three stages through which the child passes in his movement toward manhood. Sense-perception is the chief characteristic of his intellectual life in infancy, memory and imagination become active in childhood, thinking and reasoning predominate in youth. Infancy is the stage of dependence. It is spent at home, because of the individual sympathy and individual supervision then required. The period of childhood in a general way may be said to extend from the fifth to the twelfth year. At the beginning of this period the child is supposed to have attained sufficient development and self-control to enable him to mingle with children outside of his own household without much personal supervision; to enable him to take care of himself under ordinary circumstances; and to warrant his being sent to school. Youth begins with the pubescent period, at about the age of twelve. Independence and restlessness under restraint manifest themselves here more em-

195

phatically than in either preceding period. The
new impulses which the radical physical changes
at this time beget start the youth into new lines
of inquiry and investigation, not infrequently developing irreverence, heedlessness, selfishness, and
disobedience to an unfortunate degree. The
grades in the public schools most difficult to govern are those embracing children from eleven to
fourteen years of age.

Each of these three periods has several other
characteristics peculiar to itself which observation
will reveal. The way in which the child adjusts
himself to the new environment as he leaves home
to enter the schoolroom is an interesting and instructive study. This is one of the critical periods
of his life, and for the successful transition discreet management is imperative. In many cases
the approach of the pubescent period may be discovered through the mental changes in the child,
even before the physical changes are manifest.
The dispositions of infancy and childhood, whether good or bad, now usually become positively
prominent, and character more clearly defines.
Some surprising changes in mental power also
occur. A child with a poor memory may suddenly show rare ability in remembering things;
one sluggish in perception throughout childhood
may become apt in discernment: one with a vivid
imagination may become indifferent and prosy:
one of habitually happy disposition may show
symptoms of discontent or melancholy. If the
transition be healthy and natural, the intelligent
education and training of infancy and childhood

begin at once to show results in superior judgment, in clear moral conceptions, and in a well-
balanced will. These three stages in the child's
development can not be definitely assigned to the
limits mentioned, but they are sufficiently approximate to assist parent and teacher to a better
understanding of the more critical years in the
child's life and to suggest the need for a thorough
understanding of ways and means adapted to each
stage.

Children's ideals and motives are constantly
changing and methods of instruction and of management must change with them. Many a youth
is alienated from his father because his father does
not understand him. He has failed to note that
the child is a child no longer, but that he is reaching up into manhood and is thinking and reasoning for himself; that he is on that account entitled
to have his own views and preferences heard with
reasonable consideration. Many a youth goes out
into the world for the sympathy and fellowship
that are denied him at home.

The stage of the child's development should
control in the administration of punishment. In-
discriminate punishment is worse than the indis-
criminate use of medicine, however bad that may
be. The old idea that retribution should be the
controlling aim in the punishment of children is
as cruel as it is unreasonable. That idea with very
little suggestion comes into more or less prominence in the mind of the child anyhow. Punishment should in general be administered for the
purpose of quickening the child's perception of

right and wrong and of assisting him to resist temptation. Children err more often from lack of discernment than from lack of desire to do right. They are only learning what is right and what is wrong. Their characters are in the formative state and the spirit of helpfulness should always govern the inculcation of motives, whether through the positive forces of instruction and guidance or through the negative force of punishment. As a means of correction, punishment should serve for a temporary purpose only. The great and ever-active forces in character-building are sympathy and counsel, not punishment, as already explained in the chapter on Manners and Morals. Methods of correction which are slowly driving the child away from parent or teacher are their own condemnation. Nothing but that intimate acquaintance with the individual child demanded in the foregoing chapters will suffice for the wise determination of the necessity for punishment and of the kind of punishment that will prove most effective. Differences in disposition, in physical temperament, in sex, in stage of development, in home life, in previous education, in motive, etc., should control in all cases. There is, unfortunately, a widespread tendency to set up a multitude of little rules, for whose infraction the children are punished as impulse prompts. A late report shows that probably five times as many punishments, great and small, are inflicted as a result of a petty whim or for the violation of rules of propriety as for violation of the weightier laws embraced in the Ten Commandments. Children are far more reasonable than is generally supposed; if this be kept in mind, the problem of punishment solves with less difficulty.

The fatigue point is a profitable subject in child study. It has already been incidentally mentioned in connection with the eye. If you look for a few moments at a small red spot on a light-colored object and then look at a white surface, you will see a green spot of about the same shape and size as the former. This phenomenon is explained by the fact that in looking intently at the red spot the capacity of the nerve cells for appreciating the red color is slightly exhausted, while their capacity to appreciate the green, its complementary color, is not called into exercise at all. When the eye turns to the white surface, the capacity to appreciate the green being more acute, it promptly brings that color into prominence at the expense of the red. The regular *tick*, *tick*, of the clock becomes *tick*, *tack*, because of the slight difference in the exhaustive effects upon the auditory nerve cells. The sense of taste may grow temporarily obtuse to any substance because its nerve cells also become weary from the demands made upon them. This law of fatigue governs every organ of the body, including the muscles and the whole cerebro-spinal system. Rest and sleep are as necessary to the child's health and development as exercise. It is doubtful whether he can get too much sleep in infancy; few take too much in childhood. Both rest and sleep have a higher purpose than simply to relieve the child of his sense of weariness. Weariness is but a sign by which Nature gives notice that strength is disappearing, and that tissues must be rebuilt and restored. That is a heartless taskmaker indeed, who ignores the law of fatigue in the management of children.

Weariness seems to be chronic with some children. It is often said of a certain child or of a certain man, "He was born tired." Such people are more probably afflicted with laziness which may or may not be inherited. Inquiry will show you, however, that there are some genuine cases of chronic weariness among children, due possibly to weak constitutions, to lung trouble, to heart affection, to nervous depression, to lack of vitality, to continued overexertion, to lack of nourishing food, to lack of exercise, to worry, or to some kindred cause. All these cases appeal at once for kinder consideration than is usually given, but healthy children make the same appeal. It is no more important that the former be made healthy and vigorous than that the latter be kept so. Some children naturally tire more quickly than others. It ought not to be expected that all children should do an equal amount of work in the same time any more than that all should be able to lift equal weights. Work done represents just so much strength used. If all must do the same work, it means that some must be under a high tension and that others must be doing less than they are able. *The child should be required to do no more than that which he can do without overexertion, and which will gradually develop additional power from day to day.* Excessive weariness at any time means that the work has been

too heavy for the child or that it has been continued too long. Frequent rest periods and variety in work are demanded by every child.

It matters little whether the work assigned be
physical or mental. The brain tires as well as
any other part of the body. Some kinds of brain
work are more exhaustive than others. Statistics
show that school programs which ignore the law
of fatigue are most wasteful in results. Dr.
W. O. Krohn has tested about forty thousand
children with reference to the period of the day
when memory is most retentive. He found that
if the subjects were taken indifferently during the
first school hour of the day, the average retentive
power of the pupils was eighty-nine per cent; for
the last hour of the morning, sixty-three per cent;
for the first hour of the afternoon, seventy-five
per cent; for the last hour in the afternoon, sev-
enty-seven per cent. This shows very conclusively
that memory is twenty-six per cent more effective
during the first morning hour than during the
last. When the order of the subjects was reading, grammar, arithmetic, geography, and history,
the average was eighty-nine, fifty-eight, sixty-
eight, and seventy-six per cent respectively; when
the order was arithmetic, elementary science, reading, drawing, geography, and history, the average
was eighty-nine, seventy-nine, eighty-two, and
eighty-six per cent. This last arrangement of
studies increases the retentive power of the average pupil over that of the hit-or-miss program
sixteen per cent for the third hour, seven per cent
for the fourth, and nine per cent for the last hour

of the day. In other words, a rational arrangement of the school program increases the memory
power of the children from ten to twelve per cent
for the day as a whole—*a saving of one year in ten
in the school life of the child by this means alone.*
Accuracy and attention tests by other investigators
show approximately the same results, though the
inquiries have been confined within narrow limits.
In collating data on these questions many errors
creep in, but the figures are sufficiently definite
to show how fruitful in results to the home and
the school further inquiries may prove. Of course,
the program problem is not to be solved by memory tests alone. Some one is yet to do the children a great service in determining specifically the
most profitable study and recitation hours for the
different subjects.

A study of the child which ignores the æsthetic
instinct would be incomplete. Art realizes itself
in expression, or, possibly better, art is expression.
Its finer forms are poetry, music, architecture,
sculpture, drawing, and painting. In their earlier
stages they evidently served a utilitarian purpose,
or at most served to give tangible expression to
commonplace ideas. The beautiful forms in nature kindled impulses to imitate them, and æsthetic taste slowly developed, becoming more discriminating and more refined with each succeeding generation. In some such way the child
begins and progresses in drawing and painting.
The first or the hundredth picture may be very
crude indeed to us, but it is perfect to him, for it
expresses an idea. As long as it symbolizes that

to him, it has a mission. Read a story to the children, asking them all to draw pictures of the most interesting parts of it. The collection will show the points in the story most vividly affecting them, and will probably demonstrate the fact that the intellectual rather than the æsthetic activities dictate the kinds of pictures they draw. These drawings will also help you to discover the indications of artistic promise among your pupils. It is probable, though, that in most of the children the emotions of the beautiful are aroused through music and song long before they are perceptibly responding to color and form.

The harmony of knowledge and experience is called truth; the harmony or agreement of truth, as ideal, with concrete forms is called beauty; the harmony of truth and personal action is called right. The intimate relationship of the beautiful with the true and the good makes its cultivation essential to the highest attainments in the other two. In the properly educated child the pleasures of the higher senses gradually displace those of the lower, and in their turn they become subordinated to the pleasures of the intellectual life. The fine arts, appealing as they do directly to the senses of hearing and sight, thus become a powerful factor in developing the finer instincts of the child's nature. They stimulate the imagination and quicken all the higher activities of the self. For this reason every child should be surrounded with beautiful things of nature and of art. The home, however humble, should be architecturally a model, inside and out; its furniture, though plain, should be in good taste, both in design and arrangement; the yard should be beautified by ornamental shrubs and trees, flowering plants contributing their wealth of color to the scene. Such a home costs no more than the ungainly looking boxes which many people set up in barren plots and call a house and its educative effect is beyond estimate. With books on the shelves and pictures on the walls selected with the same taste and judgment, though they be few, the ideal home environment is complete, provided always that a consecrated mother's heart warms every nook and corner in it. What is desirable in the home is, in its way, also desirable in the schoolhouse. All the forces that can be brought to conspire for the cultivation of the æsthetic sense will contribute also to the making of gentler, truer manhood. Superintendent Powell, of Washington, says that since manual training, including drawing, clay modeling, and simple designing, have been introduced into the city schools, many ill-kept and degraded homes have been revolutionized both in appearance and morals. The children take matters into their own hands and become the schoolmasters of their parents, transforming repulsive hovels into cozy, inviting homes. It is an easy step from beauty of form and beauty of language to beauty of thought and action, for they are always mutually strengthening and refining each other.

The unconscious or subconscious influences that alike affect the child and the man are not less powerful in shaping the child's tastes and character than those coming consciously into his life.

The atmosphere of his environment permeates every fiber of his being, giving him tone and temperament that long years of effort can not entirely overcome. Waldstein says that the essentials in education are "about the same among all civilized nations, and that the conscious self is substantially the same wherever schools and colleges exist." The subconscious self, however, which is "built up out of that countless multitude of subconscious impressions from the surroundings, customs, language, national types, physical effects of climate, and many other sources is widely different." So effective and yet so subtle are these subconscious forces in infancy and childhood in organizing this fundamental self that doubtless much is attributed to heredity which really owes its existence to them. Conscious imitation is always accounted a great factor in education. In these earlier years unconscious imitation is continually reacting upon the child and molding him after the pattern of those with whom he constantly associates. After I had reached manhood I traveled for nearly a month with a friend who lisped in speaking certain words. Afterward, to my surprise, I found myself lisping a little, and it was years before I was entirely free from it. A distinguished professor in a Western college stammers slightly; so did his father, and so does every one of his five children. There seems to be no physical reason for it. May it not be due wholly to subconscious imitation? One of the most popular teachers of English in the West tells me that she is constantly fighting the influence of the incorrect language of her pupils upon her own language. To this principle is due the fact that a child who reads only books written by masters of diction unconsciously perfects himself in literary style. For all practical purposes, a few years of such reading is worth more than a set course in rhetoric. How important, then, that every book put into the hand of the child, whether at home or in the schoolroom, be the most perfect book on the subject that the genius of man has created! The relation of these subconscious elements to knowledge was discussed in connection with the *sensation continuum* in Chapter VIII, and it is hoped that their function in education has been sufficiently emphasized in several places to prevent their being overlooked by any reader of this book.

The function of sympathy in the care and culture of children has been recognized ever since Eve named her firstborn, but its unselfish exercise is not so general as its antiquity would warrant us to expect. The social instinct finds its most grateful satisfaction in sympathy, in the consciousness of being the object of disinterested affection and interest. The child as naturally responds to sympathy as does the plant to moisture and sunshine. Many even of his physical impulses await the encouragement of sympathy. His intellectual and moral impulses still more fully depend upon it. Whatever contributes to the child's pleasure attracts him, and its unconscious influence upon him is assured. The greatest direct educative force that can be brought to bear upon the child is sympathy; that sympathy which counts no sacrifice too great that may result in good to him; that sympathy which prompts an exhaustive study of his nature and of the various forces by which he may attain to the stature of the highest manhood; that sympathy that goes out alike to the rich and the poor, to the favored and the ill-favored, to the keen-witted and the dullard, to the faithful and the faithless; that sympathy which is long-suffering and kind, which endureth all things, which never faileth. Sympathy is the mother of patience and the inventor of devices. Its touch never chills, its resources never fail. If the study of the child does not quicken affection and interest for it, you are not called to its service, either as parent or teacher. If you are not moved to give it the best of your life, your work must in large measure be vain. The great teachers have ever been men and women of warm hearts and of unselfish devotion.

17

CHAPTER XXIII.

CONCLUSIONS.

If this book accomplishes its purpose, you are now fairly well prepared to enter upon the study of the child, for what has been said is intended simply to serve as an introduction to child nature and child problems. Many subjects discussed, as well as others not mentioned at all, are treated quite exhaustively in a scientific way by expert investigators, and their assistance will be found of much value upon any line which may attract you. (See the brief bibliography on pages 211 to 215.)

The following additional topics are among those worthy a full chapter in any book on the child: The religious ideas of children, the sense of humor in children, the indications of genius, the tendency to deterioration, curiosity and wonder, the different intellectual activities as affected by race, reaction time, the artistic sense, illusions, dreams, hypnotic suggestions, the origin of fear, the child as the child's teacher, the pubescent period, the effect of idleness, mental differences of the sexes, prejudices of children, spinal curvature, its causes and remedies. children's pranks, children's ideas of number, children's drawings, children in

storyland, books for children, the Sunday afternoon problem, the poetry and music adapted to
child life, the function of fairy tales, the true
office of the home.

Local clubs for child study are wonderful aids
to its effectiveness. Each club of teachers will
find the interest and profit greatly enhanced by
enlisting the co-operation of specialists within its
circle. Physicians, dentists, oculists, neurologists,
nurses, ministers, psychologists, scientists, and authors are usually pleased to be asked for papers or
addresses on subjects coming within the range of
their experience. A few intelligent mothers will
make invaluable members. The program at such
club meetings should include reports on personal observations and investigations. It should
bear a logical sequence to its predecessor, and the
discussions should not drift off into aimless and
profitless generalities. A review of many subjects
as outlined in this book will make a good year's
work for a club. The tendency common in some
clubs to spend most of the time in research concerning abnormal children is unwise. It is imperative that the normal child be made the center of
the study and that he be the model to which all
the others shall be conforming in their development. It is equally unwise for experiments and
tests to be conducted in such a way as to destroy
the naturalness of the child or to excite self-consciousness unduly, or to mention little peculiarities
that by the attention thus given them become less
easy for the children to outgrow. Follow the
methods of the wise physician in it all.

Mothers' clubs, composed exclusively of mothers, are forming in some localities. The zest with which they enter upon the study of these problems shows that the homes of our land as well as the schoolrooms are soon to receive the direct benefit of this great movement. The ideal condition in education is to be realized when intelligent teachers and intelligent mothers are cordially cooperating in the training of the children.

BIBLIOGRAPHY.

A COMPLETE list of books and of articles on the child and directly related subjects would itself make a small volume. The following named will be found of great value to the general as well as to the special student:

Apperception. Karl Lange. D. C. Heath & Co.

Body and Mind. Henry Maudsley. D. Appleton & Co.

The Growth of the Brain. H. D. Donaldson. Charles Scribner's Sons.

Boyhood of Great Men. J. G. Edgar. Harper Brothers.

Brain Work and Overwork. H. C. Wood, Jr. P. Blakiston, Son & Co.

Children's Ways. James Sully. D. Appleton & Co.

The Child and Childhood in Folk Thought. Alexander F. Chamberlain. Macmillan & Co.

Children of the Poor. Jacob A. Riis. Charles Scribner's Sons.

Studies of Childhood. James Sully. D. Appleton & Co.

The Child, its Spiritual Nature. Henry K. Lewis. Macmillan & Co.

Children's Rights. Kate D. Wiggin. Houghton, Mifflin & Co.

Child Study Monthly. W. D. Krohn and Alfred Bayliss, editors, Chicago.

First Three Years of Childhood. Bernard Perez. E. L. Kellogg & Co.

The Study of Children. Francis Warner. Macmillan & Co.

Dependent, Defective, and Delinquent Classes. Charles R. Henderson. D. C. Heath & Co.

The Education of the Central Nervous System. Reuben P. Halleck. Macmillan & Co.

The Eyesight and How to Care for it. Charles H. Burnett. P. Blakiston, Son & Co.

The Family, an Historical and Social Study. Charles F. Thwing. Lee & Shepard.

Habit and Instinct. Lloyd Morgan. Edwin Arnold, London.

Hearing and How to Keep it. Charles H. Burnett. P. Blakiston, Son & Co.

Heredity. Th. Ribot. D. Appleton & Co.

Hereditary Genius. Francis Galton. D. Appleton & Co.

The Hygiene of the Eye in School. Hermann Cohn. Simpkin, Marshall & Co., London.

The Intellectual and Moral Development of the Child. G. Compayré. D. Appleton & Co.

The Jukes. R. L. Dugdale. G. P. Putnam's Sons.

Juvenile Offenders. W. D. Morrison. D. Appleton & Co.

Mental Affections in Childhood and Youth. Langdon Down. J. A. Churchill, London.

* Mentally Deficient Children. G. E. Shuttleworth. H. K. Lewis, London.

Mentally Feeble-minded Children. Fletcher Beach. J. A. Churchill, London.

Mental Development of the Child. W. Preyer. D. Appleton & Co.

The Moral Instruction of Children. Felix Adler. D. Appleton & Co.

Methods of Mind Training. Catharine Aiken. Harper Brothers.

The Northwestern Journal of Education. J. H. Miller, editor. J. H. Miller, Lincoln, Nebraska.

The Pedagogical Seminary, vols. i, ii, and iii. Valuable articles on nearly every phase of the subject. G. Stanley Hall, editor. J. H. Orpha, Worcester, Massachusetts.

The Physiology of the Senses. John G. McKendrick and William Snodgrass. Charles Scribner's Sons.

Practical Lessons in Psychology. W. O. Krohn. The Werner Company.

Proceedings of National Educational Association. Papers in child study and other departments in volumes for 1894, 1895, 1896, and 1897.

Psychology and Psychic Culture. Reuben P. Halleck. American Book Company.

Psychology. John Dewey. Harper Brothers.

Responsibility in Mental Disease. Henry Maudsley. D. Appleton & Co.

The Subconscious Self. Louis Waldstein. Charles Scribner's Sons.

Symbolic Education. Susan E. Blow. D. Appleton & Co.

The Mind of the Child, vol. i. The Senses and the Will, vol. ii. Development of the Intellect. W. Preyer. D. Appleton & Co.

Studies in Education. Earl Barnes. Leland Stanford Junior University.

Studies in Home and Child Life. Mrs. S. M. I. Henry. Fleming H. Revell Company.

Transactions of the Illinois Society for Child Study. The Werner Company.

Valuable articles on the subject of child study have been published recently in nearly all the great educational periodicals. The following papers by Oscar Chrisman, Ph. D., of the State Normal School of Kansas, will repay perusal: Secret Language of Children, Science, vol. xxii, p. 303, and vol. xxiii, p. 18; The Hearing of Children, Pedagogical Seminary, vol. ii, p. 397; Child Study, a New Department of Education, Forum, vol. xvi, p. 728; One Year with a Little Girl, Educational Review, vol. ix, p. 52; Children's Secret Language, Child Study Monthly, vol. ii, p. 202; How a Story affected a Child, Child Study Monthly, vol. ii, p. 650; The Hearing of School Children, Northwestern Monthly, vol. viii, p. 31; Motor Control: its Nature and Place in the Physical and Psychical Life of the Child, State Normal Monthly, vol. x, p. 3; The Secret Language of Children, Northwestern Monthly, vol. viii, pp. 187, 375, 550; Exceptionals, State Normal Monthly, vol. x, p. 51; The Religious Ideas of a Child, Child Study Monthly, vol iii, p. 516; Paidology, the Science of the Child, Educational Review, vol. xv, p. 269; The Results of Child Study, Education, vol. xviii, p. 323; The Secret Language of Children, Century Magazine, vol. lvi, p. 54; Religious Periods in Child Growth, Educational Re-Review, vol. xvi, p. 39.

THE END.